THE PRIMITIVE TRIBES OF ANDAMAN & NICOBAR ISLANDS

THE PRIMITIVE TRIBES OF ANDAMAN & NICOBAR ISLANDS

Dr. Pronob Kumar Sircar

AKANSHA PUBLISHING HOUSE
NEW DELHI

AKANSHA PUBLISHING HOUSE
R 37-B, Vani Vihar, Uttam Nagar
New Delhi-110059
Email: ektabooks@yahoo.com
Ph. : 56065579 / 9811582579

THE PRIMITIVE TRIBES OF ANDAMAN & NICOBAR ISLANDS

First Edition 2004
ISBN 81–87606–52-5

PRINTED IN INDIA

Published by M.P. Misra for Akansha Publishing House, New Delhi and Printed at Mehra Offset Press, Delhi.

Preface

"Who am I."? Every thinking man asks himself that question at one time or another.

The search for the pre-history of human races began like so much else in science, as an aspect of man's insatiable curiosity. Within the last decades extensive new fossils and archaeological evidences have thrown valuable light on the whole process of man's evolution.

The Andaman islands are inhabited by the pure negrito blood, members of perhaps the most ancient race remaining on the earth and standing closest to the primitive human type. In the Andaman Kitchen middens have been found shells, pig bones, pottery (referred to a stone age –at least to the Neolithic period –and almost identical with the fragments found in the Danish kitchen-middens and stone implements).These unique foragers are surviving at present at the different stages of life and civilization. The Sentinelese are perhaps the most isolated community in the world while the Great Andamanese are perhaps the smallest community in the world. The Onges are perhaps the happiest looking people of the world and the Jarawas are unpredicted people. On the other hand in the Great Nicobar Island Shompens are the primitive tribes who still live semi-nomadic primitive life. Their camping in difficult and remote terrain in the island makes it difficult for us to contact them in an easy way.

The tribal areas were the last to come under the British power because of their difficult terrain and inaccessibility in mainland India but with reference to the tribes of Andaman and

Nicobar Islands, the aborigines were the first to come under the British influence. Prior to Independence the British and Japanese policy of isolation left the tribals to themselves and almost no effort was made to develop them except some efforts to contact and befriend them mainly to gain security, peaceful colonization and administration. After Independence several welfare schemes have been undertaken for the protection, survival and growth of the primitive tribes of the isles by the local administration with formation of an autonomous organization called "Andaman Adim Janjati Vikas Samiti" in March 1976 to look after the primitive tribes at the ground level.

Dr. Pronob Kumar Sircar

Acknowledgements

At the very outset I feel myself sincerely indebted to the officers of Andaman and Nicobar Administration for their co-operation in my work. At this juncture I must remember my life-master Prof. Yashwant G Joshi, Head of the Department of Development of SC/ST & OBC, Dr. Babasaheb Ambedkar National Institute of Social Sciences, Mhow (Indore), M.P. for his boundless inspiration and care.

I am highly indebted to all the staffs of AAJVS and Directorate of Tribal Welfare, Port Blair for helping me in my work from time to time.

This time, I especially remember my friends who extended their all possible supports in this work. It becomes my moral duty to pay my sincere acknowledgement.

I am highly indebted to Shri M.P. Misra, Akansha Publishing House, New Delhi for accepting my work to publish well in time.

Finally, I remember my family members for their eternal love and care.

Dr. Pronob Kumar Sircar

Contents

Preface v

Acknowledgements vii

1. Introduction 1
2. The Origin and History 7
3. The Primitive Tribes 27
4. The Welfare Activities for the Primitive Tribes 107
5. Development of Primitive Tribes—The Conceptual Frame 126

Index 134

1

Introduction

The Andaman and Nicobar Islands in Bay of Bengal, though forming one administrative unit, consist of two separate groups of Islands with entirely different populations living under very dissimilar conditions, each with its own kind. The Andaman and Nicobar groups comprising of 572 Islands, islets and rocks are located at a distance of more than 1200 kilometres from the Mainland, north to south in the Bay of Bengal. The Islands have a natural coverage of evergreen tropical rain forests up to 86% and have tremendous scope for development of international tourism.

The Andaman consists of a chain of islands stretching from Land Fall Island in the north to Little Andaman in the South in an arc stretching over 200 miles of sea. There is then an open stretch of water for 80 miles until Car Nicobar is reached, the Northern most of the Nicobar group of Islands which continue in the same arc for another 200 miles to Great Nicobar which is only about a 100 miles from the northern tip of Sumatra – less than the distance between Agra and Delhi.[1]

The Andaman and Nicobar archipelago is in form of a broken chain from North to South between Cape Negrais of Myanmar in north and Achinhead of Indonesia in South. The Archipelago is situated in the Bay of Bengal between 6° and 14° North latitude and 92° and 94° East longitude.

The geographical and geological evidences lead us to assume that the Andaman and Nicobar Islands were as parts of range from Myanmar to Sumatra. These were parts of Aracan Yoma range of present Myanmar.

The total geographical area covered by Andaman and Nicobar Islands is 8249 sq. km. The Andaman districts have an area of 6408 sq. km while the Nicobar district covers 1841 sq. km Out of the total area of these islands 16.64 sq. km is urban and 8232.36 sq. km is rural.

Port Blair, the Capital of this Union Territory has a distance of 1255 km from Calcutta and 1190 km from Chennai by sea. As far as climate of the isles is concerned, normally annual rainfall at Port Blair is more than 3000 mm. The temperature varies from 23° C to 25° C in the islands from time to time. The relative humidity is experienced about 78%. The total area of Andaman and Nicobar Islands have 2929 sq. km of reserve forest and 4242 sq. km of protected forest. There is a preponderance of evergreen trees in the Andaman forests, but they are generally heavily laden with climbers. Glades of bamboo can be found in the forests. The creeps are richly covered with mangrove forests. According to the *Imperial Gazetteers* (1908), the timber could for commercial purposes be divided into three classes. First class Padauk, Koko, Chuglum, Marble wood and Satin wood; second class Pyinma, Bombway, Chai, Lakuch, Lalchini, Pongyet, Thitmin. Mowha, Khaya, Gangaw, Thingan and third class Didu, Ywegy, Thoungpeingyi and Gurjan. The variety and wealth of the flora found in the Andaman Islands is evident from the fact that, C.E. Parkinson deals with as many as 650 plants in his book *A Forest Flora of Andaman Island.* Of them 540, he thinks are indigenous to the islands. In economic value the forests of Nicobars are less richer than that of Andamans. Pandanus, coconut, and betelnut are found abundantly in Nicobars. With coastline of almost 2000 km an Exclusive Economic Zone (EEZ) consisting of 6 lakh sq. km of marine water and some of India's richest rainforests the Andaman and Nicobar Islands are the repository of immense variety of ecosystem and wildlife. In spite of the fact that the biological investigation of the islands are far from complete, the tally of species and subspecies belong to each class / group of plants and animals is impressive over 2200 flowering plants and 120 firns (besides other plants), 58 mammals, 242 birds, 83 reptiles, 10 amphibians, 750 fishes, 320 coelenterates (Corals, sponges, sea anemoner, jelly fish etc.), 407 crustaceans (crabs, lobsters, shrimps, barnacles, etc.), 941 molluscs (Limpets, oysterns, clams, quails, slugs, squid mussels etc.), 1500 insects, 62 spiders and scorpions etc. There is a great importance of many of these described species of plants and animals in the tribal life. The tribals subsist on the several unknown and known species and subspecies belonging to each class / group of plants and animals. So far 179 species of corals belonging to 61 genera have been reported.

In these islands coastal ecosystem is being maintained by mangrove forests. These islands alone account for 18% of the country's total mangrove area. The major species of mangrove forests, include Rhizophora mucronate, which occurs in the Andamans and Bruguiera conjugata which occurs in the Nicobars.

For construction and management of wildlife in these islands provisions of Indian Forest Act 1927, Wildlife (Protection) Act, 1972, Environment (Protection) Act,1986, Coastal Regulation Zone Rules, 1991, A&N Wildlife Protection Rules 1973, and other relevant Act and Rules are enforced.

A number of species found here are 'Endangered Species' and are scheduled in Schedule I of Wildlife Protection Act, 1972. These species are given special status for protection and conservation. Some of these are: Andaman Wild Pig (*Susscorfa andamanensis*), Crabeating macaque (*Macaca fascicularis* umbrosa), Dugong (*Dugong dugon*), Elephant, Salt Water Crocodile (*Crocodylus porosus*), Leather Back Turtle (*Dermochelys coriacea*), Green Sea Turtle (*Chelonia mydas*), Hawks Bill Turtle (*Eretmochelys imricata* squamata), Olive Ridley Turtle (*Lepidochelys olivacea*), Reticulate Python (*Python reticulatus*), Andaman Teal (*Anas gibberifrons*), Narcondum Hornbill (*Rhyticeros narcondami*), Nicobar Pigeon

(*Caloenas nicobarica nicobarica*), Nicobar Megapode (*Megapodius freycinet*), White Bellied Sea Eagle (*Haliaeetus leucogaster*), etc.

There are 96 wildlife sanctuaries, 09 National Parks and One Biosphere Reserve.

Some important protected areas are –

1 Mahatma Gandhi Marine National Park.

2 Mt. Harriet National Park.

3 Saddle Peak National Park.

4 Galathea National Park.

5 Campbell Bay National Park.

6 Narcondum Island Sanctuary.

7 Cuthbert Bay Sanctuary.

8 Interview Island Sanctuary.

9 Loha Barrack Crocodile Sanctuary.

10 Battimalve Island Sanctuary.

11 Reef Island Sanctuary, and

12 Great Nicobar Biosphere Reserve.

Since the census year 1901 when the total population of Andaman Nicobar Islands was only 24,649 in number, the population of this Union Territory has been increased to 356,265 in number in 2001 (as per census report) with the large growth variation of the population in 2001. The sex ratio is 846 females per thousands males. Literacy is 81.18 per cent.

The islands are mountain peaks which have emerged from the sea. They are part of a submerged mountain range related to the Arakan Yoma Range of Myanmar. Barring Little Andaman and a few islands in Nicobars, the land is undulating with hills and ridges. The islands are very narrow with an average width of only 20 km. There are a few perennial streams. Two known volcanic islands exist here – Barren (erupted in 1991) and

Narcondum (considered extinct). The islands are heavenly beautiful endowed with rich natural resources in full virginity.

Table 1: Tehsil-wise population of Andaman and Nicobar Islands (1981 and 1991 census)

Sl. No.	Tehsil	Population (1981)	Population (1991)	*% Variation*
1.	Diglipur	15,702	23,734	+ 51.15
2.	Mayabunder	13,954	21,570	+54.58
3.	Rangat	24,289	33,368	+ 37.38
4.	Port Blair	76,329	1,23,504	+ 61.80
5.	Ferrargunj	28,031	39,277	+ 40.21
6.	Nancowrie	14,968	19,872	+ 32.76
7.	Car Nicobar	15,486	19,336	+ 24.86

Source : Statistical Bureau, A & N Administration, Port Blair.

Table 2: Geographical Distribution of the Primitive tribes in Andaman and Nicobar Islands

Sl. No.	Tribal Group	Area (sq. km)	Name of the Area
1.	Onges	731.5	Dugong Creek and South Bay in little Andaman Island
2.	Shompens	865	Great Nicobar Island.
3.	Great Andamanese	3.11	Strait Island.
4.	Jarawas	765	West Coast region of South and Middle Andaman.
5.	Sentinelese	60	North Sentinel Island.

The monsoon climate of the Andamans is generally hot and humid, often oppressively so. Heavy though rainfall can be, it is quite unpredictable from year to year and can fall most unevenly within a small area. During the time December to March temperature and humidity tend to be lower and there is less rain but it would be exaggeration to call it a "Dry" season. Violent thunderstorm occurs during the wet south – west monsoon from mid-May to end-September while tropical revolving storms (in other parts of the world known as typhoon/ hurricanes) are not directly affecting the islands. The rain, wind and the weather have strongly occupied their places in the aboriginal myths, legends, and beliefs.

There are five primitive tribes in Andaman and Nicobar Islands, viz. Shompens, Jarawas, Sentineleses, Onges and Great Andamanese. These tribes can be divided into two racial stocks. The Shompens belong to Mongoloid racial stock while the rest tribal communities belong to Negrito race. The said primitive tribal communities are at different stages of life and assimilation.

2

The Origin and History

Despite their coral reefs, most Andaman islands themselves are not of coral origin. Instead they are the peaks of a drowned mountain range. The islands lie parallel to a geographical fault line to east, crossing the Andaman sea from north to south. The line marks two tectonic plates rubbing against each other: the eastern plate, an extension of the huge Eurasian Plate, is stationary, while the Indian Plate to the west is moving north to northeast at the rate of a few centimetres a year, carrying the Andaman islands with it. This slow but steady movement is still pushing up the Himalayan mountains and causes earthquakes and volcanic activities in and around the islands. India's only active volcanoes on Barren and Narcondum Island (now believed to be dead) are sitting directly on the faultline. The present geological era is Cenozoic. It started around 65 millions years ago with an end of the Cretaceous period. Modern humans, including the Andamanese, developed during the later part of the Pleistocene, i.e. very recently on the geological time scale. The oldest rock formations represent deposits laid down in the deep, open sea from the Cretaceous period immediately proceeding the Cenozoic to the middle Tertiary. The islands were born when the sea floor, consisting of a core of fault line sand stone and shell) was lifted and piled up into the present mountain chain during the Oligocene. Richie's archipelago, Little Andaman and the Nicobars rose from the sea at a somewhat later stage. The large main islands (apart from the North Sentinel Island, Ritchie's archipelago and Little Andaman) are collectively called the Great Andamans.

Owing to the ancient course of trade, the existence of the islands has been well known from early times. Ptolemy's *Agathon daimonos nesos* probably preserves a misunderstanding of some terms applied by sailors to a place in or near to the modern Andamans. Notices and travelogues of old travellers, Chinese, other Asiatic and Europeans are continuous from the seventh century A.D.; and the islands regularly appear in some different shapes on maps of contemporary known these regions from the middle ages onwards.

No one has been able to answer the question, with any degree of accuracy as to how and when the primitive tribal groups came to the Andamans. The study of kitchen-midden of the Andamanese settlements revealed that the Negritos were present at least 2000 years ago in the Great Andamans.

Some scholars are of the view that in the remote past there might have been a land connection between the islands and the mainland and that the Negritos reached the Andaman via Myanmar. Redcliff Brown offered the view that migrants from the region of lower Burma (present Myanmar) peopled either by sea or by land, the Andaman. But how and when they arrived was not clear. Lideo Cipriani suggested that the Negritos came through the Nicobar, an idea that was questioned by Dutta on the ground that " no cultural remnants of the people in some recognizable form could be found any where in the Nicobar groups of Islands.

For quite some time it was commonly believed that the aborigines of the Andaman islands were descendants of African slaves once shipwrecked while being carried on board a Portuguese ship. But most of the anthropologists have come to the firm conclusion that they are not Negros but Negritos. The Negritos seen to have the same ancestors as the Semangs of the Malacca peninsula, the Aetas of the Philippines and other oceanic people, including perhaps, the now extinct Tasmanians. Some anthropologists have found traces of the customs, which were prevalent among them when they first came into contact with our so called civilization, even among the people of Torres Strait. There is also a conjecture that the Papuan and Melanesians are Negrito, though they are perhaps crossed with either the Malaya or the Polynesians. [2]

The Andamanese are so ancient that they did not have even any kind of pattern at one stage, was revealed when, in 1952 Lidio Cipriani, an Italian anthropologist dug up a Kitchen-midden in Goalpahar in Little Andaman Island. While digging they reached depth of about 4 metres, from the top of the midden through refuse mixed with only a little earth, very easy to penetrate. Bones, shells and other objects emerged clean as if only recently rejected. The situation altered suddenly about one meter from the bottom, when the strata became hard and cemented with a mixture of ashes and earth. In this layer the shells were calcified by exposure to fire, and so fragile they could only be recovered in broken pieces. It is clear from this that when they arrived in the Andamans, the Negrito had no pottery; there are no signs of it at all in the lowest level. Among the Andamanese tribes, Jarawa communities had arrived after the Great Andamanese in these Islands because *"Jarawa"* word has been derived from the Great Andamanese language which means *"Stranger"*.

The Andamanese when the British first got to know them, were divided into 12 main tribes; they could be said to belong to three divisions—the North Indian Group, the South Andaman Group and the Onge Group of tribes. The Tribes were further sub-divided into what is known as septs, with each sept having its own leader or headman. But these divisions and subdivisions not withstanding the aborigines of the Andaman belonged to two main classified categories – Arioto (Coast dweller) and Eremtaga (Jungle dwellers) or those living in the hinterland.

In the words of M.V. Portman - In appearance ...the Andamanese men and the young women are not unpleasing, some indeed are distinctly good looking and have fine well shaped noses, thin lips small mouths even while teeth, bright sparkling eyes, and very well shaped figures. [3]

However, in spite of some important findings, the knowledge about the origin and migration of the primitive tribes is still meagre and obscure. World's best known and most mystery riddled primitive tribes are about to undergo genetic scrutiny. Locked within their genomes are the untold secrets of these once- dreaded and now fast – vanishing native people of the Andaman and Nicobar archipelago. From studies on these genes, scientists hope to wrest clues to the roots and history of the tribes, The investigations, they believe will also yield medical spin – offs for the tribes themselves and perhaps for the rest of the world too.

The origin of the tribes remains shrouded in mystery today despite countless attempts made by ancient travellers, historians, anthropologists and government officials to unveil their roots. Who were the first people to set foot on these islands? Where did they come from? Did they all arrive in one go or in succeeding migratory waves of small groups ? How are the tribes here related to population groups elsewhere in the world? Researchers in Port Blair and Hyderabad have teamed up with geneticists from New Zealand in perhaps the final attempts to find out some answers.

Scientists from the Regional Medical Research Centre (RMRC), Port Blair and Centre for Cellular and Molecular Biology (CCMB), Hyderabad have collected some four dozen blood samples from the Andamanese, Onges and the Nicobarese. The primary goal of this study of these blood samples is to find the tribe's place on the human family tree. In a triangular project the CCMB, Anthropological Survey of India and University of Otago, New Zealand have pooled their expertise to conduct genetic studies here.

In the past, genomic studies of population elsewhere in the world have revealed their historical roots and also indicated how present populations are related to each other. One study showed that the Kazhakh, Uighur and Kirghiz people of Central Asia are the descendants of those who moved from Europe to Asia and from Asia to Europe around 2000 years ago. That may not be really so surprising since Central Asia lay along the Trade route between Europe and Asia between 200 BC and 400 AD.

A genetic study has helped a tribe in southern Africa trace their history to the Middle East. The tests, based on the analysis of Y-Chromosomes showed that a tribe called the Lemba come from the Jews who migrated from Yemen to Southern Africa around 2000 years ago. More than a half of the Lemba Y-Chromosomes contain the specific sequences found in Jews but absent is neighbouring African Tribes. The Lembas of South Africa speak Bantu language, but the existing myths and legends differ the Lembas from other Bantu speaking communities. The genetic study reveals that the ancestors of Lembas actually were the Jews who migrated from Central East regions to Yemen some 2700 years ago and from Yemen to South Africa some 2000 *to* 2400 years ago. In most of the earlier studies special attention as paid to the African races in the context of the origin and migration of Andaman tribes.

The human society was having slow pace of change even in the Neolithic period. The Neolithic period is pertaining to the last period of the stone age (succeeding the Palaeolithic and Mesolithic) from about 6000 to 3000 BC in Europe and western Asia, when Neoliths came into use as well as implements of polished bone and horn, animals came to be domesticated, crops cultivated, weaving undertaken and the wheel used. The long Barrows and megaliths of Britain are associated with this cultural period. The Andaman tribes are still at the socio-economic and cultural stage where using of wheel, crop cultivation and domestication of animals have been unknown to these foragers.

In a paper published in '*Science*' in 1991 Allan C. Wilson and co-workers used human mitochondrial DNA to derive a tree of descent for humans that showed more differentiation in Africa than anywhere else. The scientists studied in two highly variable mitochondrial DNA segments from two groups of persons one consisting of Africans from Sub-Saharan population and the other of non- African: the African groups showed bigger differences in mitochondrial DNA sequences than the other groups. Since the accumulation of mitochondrial DNA mutation is a function of time, the scientists inferred that the sub Saharan population is older. Human mitochondrial DNA has been evolving a longer time in Africa than anywhere else. In fact the evidence suggests that we human share a common ancestress who lived in Africa perhaps 1,50,000 to 2,00,000 years ago.

The modern humans should have begun with a single couple or a small group that lived in Africa. That Africa was indeed the original homeland of our species is suggested not only by an independent molecular study by Luingi Luca Cavalli-Sforza at Standford University but also by the archaeological record in the form of bones and stone implement. The earliest Homosapien fossils are in Africa as the adjacent areas of the Levant.

The latest genetic researches indicate that the Andamanese have clear affinities to Asian than African populations and therefore are the descendants of early Paleolithic colonizers of south east Asia – hunter gatherers and the first migrants moved out of Africa about 60,000 to 1,00,000 years ago (Thagaraj et al. 2002). Palaeoanthropology evidences suggest that the Andaman Negrito occupied the islands at least 2000 years ago (Dutta 1974).

On the basis of her archaeological findings Zarine Cooper hold that the islanders must be regarded as active players in the arena of Andaman sea wherein lay adequate scope for the adoption and rejection of ideas and innovations. Despite being victims of slave raiders and other marauders, the islanders were by and large able to keep strangers at bay and when the occasion arose, were able to interact with them. She concludes with a note that the Andaman Island represents the dynamic interaction of traditions within and outside the Archipelago, a process that spans at least two millennia (Cooper 2002: 165-167).

HISTORY

Before the British colonists established a base in the islands in 1789 at Chatham Island there were many obscure description made by different travellers, explorer and others. As far as Nicobar is concerned it was situated along the ancient trade route and it was mentioned in different ways in Historical documents. The Nicobar Islands were described in Great Tanjore inscription of 1050 AD too. The name "*Nicobar*" has been derived from "*Nacabar*" via "*Nakkavaram*". The word Nicobar came into existence since at least 1560. Right before twenty three years (1756) of the establishment of the first colony in Andaman, Danes came to establish a colony in Nicobar.

The prime purpose of the visit by Danes was of two folds, i.e. Conversion and colonization. For the same purpose in 1778 Australians came to Nicobar but failed to achieve the goals. In 1804 Moravian missionaries had come in action for the same purpose. During the period between 1807 and 1814 the islands were in the hands of Britishers but recaptured by Danes through an accord but they could not posses the right over the lands of Nicobars for a long period. In the year 1845 and 1858 two attempts were made for colonization in Nicobar but failed. But in 1869 Britishers had established a penal settlement at Nancowry Island which was abolished in 1888. During the second world war in 1942 the Japanese had occupied the Nicobar islands title the end of world war in 1945. The Britishers reoccupied the Islands and left in 1947.

In Andamans, the first penal settlement was closed because of its malaria-infested environment and other hampering circumstances on the lives of settlers and for East India Company it was very expensive to manage the things and maintain the colony under the contemporary circumstances. During the period of existence of first penal colony the Jarawas living near the present Dandas Point and Bimblitan near the creek were not particularly affected by the colonists during the period.

The Indian Mutiny of 1857 forced the Britishers to establish a fresh penal settlement in March 1858 after the failure of the first penal settlement (1789-1796) in the islands which was administered by a British Superintendent. This designation was converted into Chief Commissioner in 1872. Edward Horace Man, son of Colonel Man hoisted the Union Jack at Port Blair on 22nd Jan, 1858, when the second settlement was founded.

The modern history of Andaman and Nicobar Islands begins with the bringing in of 200 mutineers of 1857 in January, 1858. The second groups of political prisoners to Andaman consisted of Wahabi Convicts. Quite a large number of Business of tharawadda who revolted against the British were also kept in Andaman. But these were all before building the Cellular Jail (present National Memorial). The construction of the Cellular Jail was taken up in the year 1896 on the basis of Order No. 423 dated 30th September, 1896 issued by the then Administration. This order was issued by Col. NMT Horsford, Superintendent of Port Blair. The construction of Cellular Jail was completed in 1906, when Sir Richard Temple was the Chief Commissioner. The earthquake of 1941 and the Japanese invasion followed by occupation of this territory by them caused substantial damage to the Jail building resulting in the need for demolition of 4 out of its 7 wings. When the island fell into the hands of Japanese from 23rd March, 1942 to 7th October, 1945, the prisoners and other suspected citizens were thrown under their barbarous inhuman methods. Many of them had been shot dead and many were buried in common graves. The "Humphrey Gunj Martyrs Memorial" 15 km from Port Blair today stands as a mute witness to the inhuman treatment meted out to the elite of Andaman by the Japanese on mere ground of suspicion. The Cellular Jail of national and historical importance was converted into a National Memorial by the then Prime Minister Shri Morarji Desai on 11th February, 1979.

When the second penal settlement was established on Ross Island in 1858 the adjoining area was populated by the Aka-bea tribes. The Jarawas were not directly affected by the establishment of penal settlements at the initial stage. There were frequent incidents of fighting between the Andamanese and the population of the settlement area. The most horrible and memorable fight was the Battle of Aberdeen. But before the battle of Aberdeen there were previously two major attacks made by the Great Andamanese.

The first battle by 200 Great Andamanese was organized on 6th April 1859 in which four convict workers were killed (Portman, 1899(1): 276). The second attack was made on 14th April 1859, in which 1500 Great Andamanese attacked the penal settlement killing 3 and took away 12 convicts with fetter on as "*Prisoners of war*", about whom nothing is known thereafter (Portman, 1899(1): 277-8). The third attack, which was notoriously known as "Battle *of Aberdeen", was* organized on 17th May 1859. Let us know actually what happened in the "*Battle of Aberdeen*". On April 23rd, 1858 two convicts namely Shri Doodhnath Tiwari and Shri Sadloo with 90 other convicts escaped from the British imprisonment. The remaining convicts except Shri Doodhnath Tiwari and Shri Sadloo were killed by the aborigines. As act of mercy, the tribals not only left Doodhnath Tiwari but allowed him to stay with them. Shri Doodhnath Tiwari lived with them for a year and 24 days. During May 1859 Shri Doodhnath Tiwari came to know about a communal plan of a great attack on the British camps made by the Great Andamanese. Quietly slipping away from the encampment of the aborigines in the night with Shri Sadloo (who was staying with other group of the Great Andamanese and came in contact with the Tiwari group) Shri Doodhnath Tiwari reached Port Blair and informed the then Superintendent of the convict settlement about the intention of the aborigines. As result in the fight the non-autochthons were armed with modern weapons and had a firmed protection. None of the Britishers was wounded seriously while several attacking Great Andamanese were shot down and seriously wounded. But the valour and act of patriotism to save the motherland shown by the Great Andamanese were no doubt worthy of none but a salutary respect that they deserve to receive from the people of free India.

It is interesting to note that in December 1866 Doodhnath Tiwari ex-convict No. 276 who had escaped to the jungle in April 1858 and had lived a year with the Great Andamanese, revisited Port Blair while in the service of Major Wraughton, Assistant Commissary General who stopped at Port Blair in the vessel

Arracan on his way from Calcutta (present Kolkata) to Rangoon. Homfray, Superintendent of the settlement, took Doodhnath to the Andaman Home and he was at once recognised by the Andamanese, and some of the men appeared glad to see him, though the women abused him for living them and especially for abandoning his wife when she was pregnant.

Homfray took the opportunity of his presence in the settlement to test the accuracy of Doodhnath's statements to Dr. Walker regarding his wanderings and found them to be fairly accurate. Homfray stated:

> *Dudhnath was taken by, and lived with the Labyrinth Island Sept, of whom Maia Potea, a man then about thirty five years of age, and still is the Chief (in 1866). After Doodhnath had lived with them for sometime a girl named Lipa was given to him in marriage. This woman is still alive, stout and happy and must be now about 35 years of age. Knowing that her husband Doodhnath is still alive she yet remains unattached to any Andamanese, (Portman remarked that the real reason was that none of them would have anything to do with a woman who had been the wife of a native of India, so much did they dislike outsiders.) Her title now is changed to 'Modo', signifying a deserted bride or woman who has lost her husband while young, and without becoming a mother. Maia Potea Lipa were both absent from at the time Doodhnath visited it."* (*Priten Roy and Swapnesh Choudhury, 2000:26)*

The British authorities had no clear knowledge of the separation of tribal bands from each other. Through the experiment of Andaman Home they came to know through the befriended Great Andamanese informants about the existence of the Jarawa as a group distinct from others.

During the period of the first penal settlement Colebrook (1789-90) and Capt. Blair (1789-96) came in contact with the Jarawas though their identity as a separate tribes was not clearly known to them. It is noteworthy that on basis of the report from the said two Britishers the first penal settlement in 1789 was established, on failing of which on 4th March 1858, Dr. J.P. Walker, Jail Superintendent arrived at Port Blair with four European officers and about 773 convicts to establish second penal colony. In a report it was stated that at the time of Colonel J.P. Walker's tenure of office, 64 died in the hospital, 140 escaped into the forest and were killed by the tribes, 87 had been hanged for the conviction of escape and one committed suicide.

In 1870 a school and orphanage was established on Ross Island for the benefit of the Andamanese. By 1879, large areas of the land were brought under cultivation, swamp infested lands were reclaimed sanitation and health of the population improved, roads and tanks were constructed and economic resource of the people developed. Released convicts were rehabilitated with their families in the out lying village in South Andaman and thus a free population began to spring up and the colony began to spring up and the colony began to develop in size and prosperity. In 1882 the forest department was established at Port Blair and a small saw mill was erected on Chatham Island which is perhaps the oldest saw mill in Asia. In 1890 the construction of the Cellular Jail, the Bastile of India was started and completed in 1905. There was a clustering of the population around the jail. These were in fact the foundation of the modern Port Blair town. [4]

The Jarawas and the Sentinelese maintained their existence of the unfriendly attitude towards the outsiders as a way to defend themselves from the outsiders. The Onges were also hostile to begin with but their hostility was eventually converted into friendship. Till 1867, the Onges had escaped the attention of the British because their inhabited island (Little Andaman) was virtually unapproachable. Dr. Frederic John Mouat, Chairperson of the Andaman Committee was looking for a suitable site for establishment of a penal settlement in 1857 but he did not make any attempt to land there.

In April 1867, Major Nelson Davies, Secretary to the Chief Commissioner of British Burma happened to be on a visit of inspection at Port Blair (At the time the Andaman Islands were under the administrative control of the Chief Commissioner of Burma). He had just finished his inspection and was waiting for a ship to take him back to Rangoon. The *S.S. Arracan* arrived to do so. In the mail that she brought on board was a telegram sent by the shipping agents, Messrs. Bullock Brothers in Akyab, to their office in Rangoon, which read:

> Assam Valley arrived under charge of Chief officer on 21st (in the month of March) at noon. Captain and seven of the crew ashore on the south end of Little Andaman Island to cut a spur, were seen to land and haul up the boat; an hour afterwards a crowd of natives were seen on the beach dancing. No Europeans were seen afterwards. The ship hovered about till Saturday evening, 23rd and came on here. Report to authorities. [5]

It was revealed that the said Europeans had been murdered. In rescue operation a ship namely *HMS Sylvia* under the command of Commander Brooker sailed for Onge inhabited island but Brooker could not land on the spot because of the heavy surf in the turbulent sea off Little Andaman. But the rescue team had been able to espy a coil of rope and a sailor's blue cap. In search of the crew of Assam Valley another ship "*Kwang Tung*" with Homphray, Lieutenant Duncan and few Andamanese sailed for Little Andaman but could not achieve the goal due to the frequent showering of arrows by the Onges from the shoreline. On failing of this punitive expedition a ship namely *IGS Arracan* under the command of Captain Barrow was sent to search the sailors of Assam Valley to Little Andaman Island. Captain Barrow was accompanied by two other officers Dunn and Eastwood. Homphray of course went again. Few Andamanese and a small military force of more than twenty five men were also on board in *IGS Arracan*. This party achieved success for the first time to land on the Little Andaman and come back safely to Port Blair. Except Lieutenant Glassford drowned, there was no casualty in this expedition. Seeing this expedition is the only one in British military history which resulted in five of the participants being awarded the most coveted British military award- the 'Victoria Cross'. During this expedition it was estimated that about 100 aborigines were killed, besides some estimated it around 70. Whatever the count there was no doubt that the casualties among the Onges were heavy, whereas the British lost only one man- the Volunteer Lieutenant Glassford. In addition to the award of Victoria Cross to Dr. Campbell Millis, Douglas and four privates. Tok Secunnie was awarded salary for two months and Private Wilson, a silver watch and chain.

In 1873 five crew of a Burmese ship *"Quangoon"* had landed in Little Andaman in search of water and had been murdered by the aborigines. Under the leadership of General Sir Donald Stewart an attempt was made to land on Little Andaman, but returned back with no success.

As a consequence and in retaliation, a punitive expedition under Captain Wimberly was sent to Hut Bay and the party killed a number of tribals and burnt down a number of communal huts and canoes. After this massacre, the island was not visited by any outsider until 1878.[6]

After Colonel Cadell took over as Chief Commissioner in early 1878 he and Portman (The new officer in charge of the Andamanese) accompanied by other officers and Andamanese started paying periodical visit and leave presents for the Onges for establishing friendly contact with them. The policy of capturing Onges for conversation was also adopted by the Britishers. In 1885 twenty four persons (few of whom released soon) were captured considering them as Jarawa from Great Cinque Island but they were in fact Onges. The captives were kept under the personal care of Portman. This time Portman came to know that tribal people of Little Andaman call themselves *"Onge"*.

In 1886 the Onges were for the first time came in contact with an outsider who was Portman. He became the first person in history to land on Onge land and successfully stay. He found the existence of Syphilis among the Onge.

At the end of January 1895, among those included in a 15-

man party of Andamanese being taken to Calcutta, were four Onges. Calcutta was in the grip of a small pox epidemic. They therefore saw nothing of the city, except the museum and the Zoological Garden. Of course they were received by His Excellency the Viceroy, the East of Elgin, at Government House in Kharagpur. According to Portman who took the party, they enjoyed their visit to the Viceroy's house, as they were able to get " a good view of the railways, buildings and bridges as well as the native fishing craft, etc." He does not say whether their reaction was any different from that of the other Andamanese who had been taken to Calcutta on previous occasions. [7]

In 1930 three Onges were persuaded to accompany the Census Superintendent, Mr. Bonnington to Car Nicobar along with few Great Andamanese members as guards. The Onges were frightened by the Nicobarese and as a consequence one of them fled and never returned, another jumped into the sea and drowned and the third had to be kept locked up to be released in Little Andaman.

> "The group names like Tetaje, Beriedalu, and Ingotijalo. Inge etc. have existed among the Onge for about a hundred (1888-1987) years".[8]

The first recorded Jarawa reference was made in 1790. Lieutenant Robert Hyde Colebrook made a voyage around the Andamans in 1789-90 in the company of commodore (later Sir William Cornwallis, brother of the then Governor General of India, Lord Cornwallis. Colebrook found few tribes with canoes near the present Dandas Point. Some words collected by him were later found to be of Jarawa language. This leads the fact that the Jarawa had canoes about 200 years ago but during the second penal settlement there were only Great Andamanese around the settlement region but no Jarawa surprisingly. Portman also tested some words collected by Colebrook to be of the Jarawa language.

Due to some unknown reasons the Great Andamanese became far stronger by the time of the second settlement had occupied almost the entire land around the harbour, having driven the Jarawas into the hinterland. There was frequent fighting between the two groups.

In 1863, two Jarawas were caught by Goodur, a convict Jamadar of the Homes but released after a good treatment. In December, 1875, six convicts were captured by the Jarawas and few of them were kept in captivity for about 19 days. In the following years Jarawa huts were looted, their weapons and utensils brought out on different occasions. As a sort of compensation some presents like matches, pipes, tobacco, looking glasses etc. were left in the Jarawa huts but these were unknown to the tribes.

There were several recorded and non-recorded incidents of capturing of Jarawa and fights between Jarawa and non-Jarawa occurred in British India. The Britishers in most of the fights, capture and other activities used to receive the prime assistance from the convicts and /or Great Andamanese.

On many occasions the Jarawas were captured and brought to Port Blair and sent back after few days. Many a time in the years that followed, clashes of one kind or the other took place, because it became more and more clear that the Jarawas distrusted every one, particularly the Great Andamanese.

The British paid their Andamanese trekkers with food, tobacco and alcohol. When on 25th March 1884, a Jarawa group was sighted, a fight with bows and arrows ensued. One Jarawa man was killed and another got injury in his leg. The wounded Jarawa namely Talai was taken to Port Blair. After his recovery Talai had a friendly term with Mr. Portman, Officer-in-Charge of the Andamanese. With a great hope and enthusiasm with Talai, 30 convicts and a large number of Andamanese Mr. Portman led an expedition to contact the Jarawas but all his hopes crushed when Talai quietly absented himself and disappeared. Thus the British attempts to capture the Jarawas, teach them and get them free to play role of intermediary did not work. Later on another Jarawa boy was caught and the Talai case repeated.

On a most interesting odd incident I must narrate—two Jarawas were captured on 7th April, 1885 by the Britishers with the help of Great Andamanese and victims. One captured Jarawa woman fell in love with one Great Andamanese boy namely Mark and she wanted him to go with her. Mark did not give any active response to her. This is a rare case of love between Jarawa and Great Andamanese.

Because of more forests were being cleared and more encroachments into the tribal territory, the Jarawas became unfriendly after 1901. There were murders of the convicts working in the forest on several occasions. In February, 1902 a team of Rogers, the Deputy Conservator of Forests, Bonig, assistant harbour master, Messrs Vaux, one policeman, three convicts and sixteen Great Andamanese was sent by Sir Richard Temple, the then Chief Commissioner on a punitive expedition against the Jarawa. In this expedition in the fight Mr. Vaux was died of attack by the Jarawa. All British efforts to capture the Jarawa and to befriend them went in vain to greater extent. The Jarawa raids became so daring that in 1917 a train on a tram line was held up. The Jarawa raids continued even after India received Independence and Britishers left the islands forever.

The North Sentinel Island is presently inhabited by Sentinelese but as per the historical statements of British officers, the Island was inhabited by the Jarawa. May be the present island tribes (Sentinelese) are actually Jarawa or the present Sentinelese were discovered to be Jarawa by the Britishers by mistake.

The Britishers had discovered the tribes of Rutland Island and North Sentinel Island to be of Jarawa community. In March 1867, Homphray writes:

> "I had occasion. In pursuit of runaways, to visit the North Sentinel Island, a distance of about 25 miles to the Westward of Port Mout with some Great Andamanese accompanying me. We saw some ten men on the beach, naked, long haired and with bows and arrows shooting fish. My friends told me that they were Jurrah wallahs (Jarawa men) who were not

friendly to them, having some years past encountered some of the tribe on Rutland Island in which their chief was wounded. "

North Sentinel Island was left alone for centuries and for the first time in history Portman and Cadell landed on the Island in 1880. In his second visit in the same year Portman was able to capture a woman and four small children and the tribes were released soon.

Portman as obvious from his report in 1894 had felt that the Jarawas on North Sentinel Island (?) could be tamed for scientific and other reasons.

> "Portman suggested a small policy as far as the Jarawas on Rutland Island was concerned. But there is nothing on record to show whether or not the policy or the methods suggested by him were over put into effect. However, the fact remains that the Jarawas of North sentinel Island happen to be the unfriendly of them all."[9]

Man (1886) believed that the Shompens were from the Nicobarese stock. The first time the world heard of the existence of the Shompen was in 1831 from Pastor Rosen, a Danish missionary. In 1846 Admiral Steen Bille paid the first recorded visit to Great Nicobar Island.

In 1870 M de Roepstorff paid three visits and his findings were added by the findings of Boden Kloss and Anderson. In 1901 Boden Kloss met the Shompens of different locations in Great Nicobar. In 1905 C.P.B. Anderson paid a visit to this Island. Under a search expedition in 1952 B.S. Cehngappa, the then Conservator of Forest estimated the Shompen number to be not more than 100 in his visit to Shompen locations in the year 1952. In the same year (1952) Sondhi had met the Shompen and came to know many riddles. Subsequently M.G. Rajaram (1960), M.K. Nag (1966), S. Raha (1970). S. Mukherjee (1974-75) and T. Lall (1978) had visited the Shompen area and met the Shompen successfully.

The history of contacts with the aborigines of Andaman and Nicobar Islands has many parts left untold and unwritten. In totality a real history of the islands still serves a challenge to search out and be written.

During the initial period of occupation, the British cleared some 140 acres of land for cultivation, which rose to 353 acres with an additional 724 acre of land being later deforested. Subsequently about 3000 acres of land were cleared and 876 acres were brought under cultivation. In 1869 the settlement again came under the direct control of the British Indian Government. In 1870 during the rule of Lord Mayo many convicts were given freedom of movement and were encouraged to marry convict women with the idea of settling them and expanding agriculture in the islands. With the increase in number of convict population requirement of food naturally rose and the local production of vegetable and other foodstuffs demanded an immediate expansion. Under this circumstances agriculture was encouraged in the islands in south of Port Blair. By the end of the year 1894-95, 22. 306 acres of land were cleared and 10. 140 acres of land were cultivated of which the Government plantation of tea, coffee, cocoa, coconuts and vegetables occupied 4. 425 acres and the remaining land was cultivated by convict settlements.[10]

In 1883 the Forest Department was established. The exploitation of timber from the forest was already taking place since the formation of the penal colony in these islands.

The process of development was initiated in the Andaman and Nicobar Islands by the British Indian administration from the time of the establishment of the penal settlement. The infrastructural facilities were provided mainly for the functioning of the colonial administration. The Japanese built about 22 miles of road and some industries based on locally available materials during the period of rule.

The population of Andaman and Nicobar Islands has reached about 4 lakh by now which was just 14628 in 1881. The population growth of Andamans in beginning was well contributed by Integrated Resource Development Plan (IRDP) and schemes of migration and settlement. Prior to the IRDP implementation 2,887 families from East Pakistan, 157 from Kerala, 43 from Tamil Nadu, 184 from Bihar, 4 from Mahe and 5 from Burma (Present Myanmar) had been settled in these islands. Prior to it in 1964, in the light of the recommendations made by IRDP 339 families of migrants from the erstwhile province of East Pakistan were resettled in Betapur in Middle Andaman. About 100 families with refugees from East Pakistan were settled in Neil Island. In Little Andaman by 1975, 353 families had been inducted and 104 were on their way. About 37 families were resettled in a rubber plantation in South Andaman. About 66 families of Sikhs arrived in Great Nicobar in 1969. There were about 238 families in Great Nicobar in 1975 from Punjab, Maharashtra, Tamil Nadu, Uttar Pradesh, Kerala, Karnataka and from Andhra Pradesh.[11]

As per a source the total number of convicts transported to Port Blair grew steadily from 11,440 in 1881 to 11,718 a decade later and from 11,974 in 1901 to 14,696 in 1905-06. The number of non-murder convicts was increasing and there were 4,495 such prisoners in 1881 but 6,137 in 1905-06. Since non-murder convicts were generally released into the community earlier than murder convicts Port Blair saw an emerging civil community.

Though few convict settlers brought in relatives from the mainland, possibly because of the social stigma of incarceration, an autonomous settlement was growing. While in 1874 there were just 825 administrators and 838 settlers from Bengal, the number tripled by 1901, by then 1,594 administrators were deployed in the Islands and 2,991 migrants from Bengal had made their homes. There is little reason to believe that this emerging community was systematically encouraged. Rather, the presence of economic opportunity in the form of meeting the administrators' needs and working on clearing forests were drawing immigrants from the mainland. By the end of the 19th century the islands were divided into the 'free' districts of Ross, Aberdeen, Haddo and Garacharama and the 'Convict' districts of Viper and Wimberlygunj.[12]

Since India became Independent in all respects the Andaman and Nicobar Islands were brought under all-round development process from plan to plan. A.K. Ghosh, Chief Commissioner (1952-53) to N.N. Jha, Lt. Governor (1998 onwards) there has been a chain of administrators in these islands. More than 1010 registered small scale villages and handicraft units besides a few medium sized industrial units have been established. The Andaman and Nicobar Islands Integrated Development Corporation (ANIIDCO) was established in 1988 which has been working in the fields of supplies, tourism, fisheries and industries. Presently the islands are under the full growth of factors for the development but the pace varies from one part to another in the islands for several reasons.

3

The Primitive Tribes

The Primitive tribes of Andaman and Nicobar Islands can broadly be grouped into two racial stocks viz. Negrito and Mongoloid. Jarawa, Sentinelese, Onge, Great Andamanese belong to the former stock while the Shompen belong to the latter. The Jarawa are presently inhabiting west coast forest belt of south and middle Andaman, Onges are settled at two places viz. Dugong Creek and South Bay, Great Andamanese are settled at a separate island called Strait Island and the Sentinelese defend themselves from any outside contact being on a separate island called 'North Sentinel Island'.

The total number of primitive tribes of Andaman and Nicobar Islands constitutes below 1% of the total population (2,80,661 as per 1991 Census) of Andaman and Nicobar Islands, which is really meagre. In the islands the total population in 1901 was only 24,649 which increased to 2,80,661 in 1991 with the growth variation of + 48 (70%). In the recent years the population of the island so drastically increased that as per a strong estimation it has passed the figure of four lakhs. The tribal groups were brutally dealt with at the time of British and Japanese occupation. In the mainland the tribal areas were the last to come under the British power because of their difficult terrain and inaccessibility. But with reference to the tribes of these islands they were the first to come under the British power.

Table 3: The Population of Primitive Tribes in Andaman and Nicobar Islands

Year	Total Population of A & N Islands	Onge	Great Andamanese	Jarawa	Sentinelese	Shompen
1901	24649	(672)	(1882)	(585)	(385)	(348)
1911	26459	(631)	(1317)	(114)	-	(375)
1921	27086	(321)	(786)	(114)	(117)	(375)
1931	29463	((250)	(460)	(70)	(50)	(200)
1941	33768	-	-	-	-	-
1951	30971	150	23	(50)	-	(20)
1961	63548	129	19	(500)	(50)	71
1971	115133	112	24	(275)	-	92
1981	188741	97	26	(200)	-	223
1991	280661	99	32	(200)	(250)	200
2001	(356,265)	92	43	(350)	(100)	Above 250

Note: Figures in parentheses are estimated

THE GREAT ANDAMANESE

Among the Baratang group of islands (comprising of 14 islands with approximate area of 129.25 sq miles) the Strait Island has an area of 3.11 sq km and is at present inhabited by Great Andamanese. The island is completely restricted under law for others except the authorized officials to land and enter.

The Great Andamanese are short scattered Negrito tribes of Andaman. The average height of their women and men are respectively 4' and 5' approximately. Their skin colour varies from black to dark brown. Some women were seen with heavily frizzy hairs and some are seen with long curly hairs. Their lips are not very thick. Physical damage can apparently be seen amongst them from one generation to another.

The historical picture of the Great Andamanese really is not in full accuracy and is obscure still while whatever has been documented so far is either from the scattered official documents or books or published travelogues at different intervals. During the second century A.D. Claudius Ptolemy referred to the islands as Buzacata.

Great Andamanese are most enigmatic of human races. A recent analyses of the Andamanese mitochondrial DNA has confronted their long standing isolation and has corroborated the fact that they are more closely related to the south African Khoisan (formerly known as Bushman and Hottentot) than to their Asian neighbours, making them a major new argument for the 'OUT OF AFRICA' theory of common human origin. Links to Papuans, Malenesians and Australians have also turned up in very recent research, as yet unverified and unpublished.

The incredible antiquity of their way of life and the tenacity with which they have survived through countless millennia deserve our greatest respect and sympathy.

The Andamanese hostility was not in form entirely. On some occasions recordedly the Andamanese met visiting ships happily and friendly. The slave taking by others have affected their behavioural pattern towards the outsiders. The erratic behaviour of the Aka-bea on the Interview Island was noticed. When on 1st September 1849 the ship 'Emily' was wrecked on the coast, the Andamanese behaved in classical style when they attacked the moment the survivors reached the supposed safety of the beach. The lucky crew somehow escaped in two salvaged boats. One of them reached Burma (present Myanmar) to raise the alarm. In late October the ship 'Proserpine' set off to look for the wreck of the Emily and its crew. The Proserpine discovered a looted Emily and the corpse of the Second Officer. He was obviously murdered. His body was badly mangled. In November 1849 and again in 1850 another ship 'Sea Serpent' twice visited the spot where the Emily wrecked. After failure of the first visit on the second visit the captain found oddly friendly natives. The Andamanese came into the friendly contact.

In 1771 the Surveyor, Ritchie reportedly had been on friendly terms with an Andamanese group but no details are known and the friendly group could not be identified.

Despite some occasional friendly contacts attacks on the ship wrecked peoples trying to land on shore were in normal trend of the native Andamanese. Some of the ships that wrecked on the coast of these islands were Emily (wrecked on 1st Sept. 1849), British ship Briton, an American built barque having 431 persons wrecked in Nov. 1844 and Runnymede wrecked in Nov. 1844.

Dr. Helfer's story throws some light on the behavioural pattern of so called hostile ancient Andamanese. Dr. Helfer visited the island on 20th January 1840 and made friendly contact with the natives by way of giving gifts. Dr. Helfer once again went ashore and tried to contact them but he and his followers were suddenly attacked and as result Dr. Helfer died.

During the first penal settlement the Great Andamanese were found in the areas around the settlement. Their population was at that time estimated to be above 5000. Where the Great Andaman islands were inhabited by the Great Andamanese on the other hand the Jarawas were surviving as neighbour tribes.

The Andamanese were the first people to fight against the outsiders (Britishers) on the island and also the first to come in friendly relation with the outsiders (Britishers). At the time when the Andamanese were staying with non-friendly gesture in the densed forest 'Andaman Home' was introduced by the Britishers. The Britishers started the Andaman Home to convey their message of peace and friendship to the aborigines through it but it was dubious. The Home was founded during the administration of Col. R.C. Tytler in 1863. Rev. H. Corbyn and Chaplain at Port Blair had made strong efforts to get on friendly terms with the aborigines. The captive Great Andamanese were treated well in the "Andaman Home" but the hospitality of Andaman Home was the cause for introduction of civilised vices including general diseases. They became addicted to opium and liquor and they were decimated by a series of epidemic.

Let us discuss in more detail about the role of Andaman Home in the history of Andamanese. It was established in 1863 after an islander (Tura) had been taken captive allegedly for killing a British soldier (later discussed). The British soldier was Mr. Pratt who tried to rape Great Andamanese woman. Andamanese members who came to see their fellow member were kept in detention by the Britishers in huts which were later came to be known as Andaman Home. An officer was placed in charge of the home whose duty was to over see the education of the Andamanese in the ways of civilization. To the Andamanese, the Home was in fact the home of a generous neighbour, they stayed for as long the British were able to provide them with the materials goods such as cloth, steel, tobacco, alcohol etc. they desired.

The British still considered the Home to be a success and began establishing numerous "Out Station Home" along the frontiers of the settlements which met with the same degree of success as they found at the first Homes.

Ultimately the Homes contributed to the spread of disease among the Andamanese because housing condition was cramped and unsanitary. In one case the islanders were housed in a cattle shed along with the cattle. The first reported epidemic in 1868 five years after opening of the Andaman Home involved bronchial pulmonary infections. From 1864 to 1870 the British reported 150 births in the Home; but of these children no one lived beyond two years (Census of India 1911: 78).

In February 1875 Man noticed syphilitic sores on some Andamanese staying on Andaman Home on Viper Island. Investigations revealed that these islanders had been suffering from the disease for some four years. Reportedly interim charge of the Andamanese noticed sores in January of 1875, but nothing was done to prevent its spread. Portman suggests that the disease had probably been seen in existence for six years. A Convict working at the Viper home was blamed for having spread the illness after having raped Andamanese women (Portman 1899 Vol. 2:597-607). Man tried to isolate those Andamanese infected with the disease, but they resisted being confined in the hospital and fled to the forest. At the time that syphilis had been detected at the home, it was found that all of the tribes in south and middle Andaman also were infected with the disease. To compound matters, Opthalmia (eye infection) broke out, leaving many islanders partially or completely blind. Man himself became infected with this illness (Mathur 1984:168).

In 1858 the indigenous population was estimated to be above 5000 but rapidly decreased to be 1,999 by 1901. In the midperiod the tribes succumbed to new disease which developed into severe epidemic e.g. pneumonia (1868), syphilis (1876), measles (1877) and influenza (1892).

The Penal colonies for the Great Andamanese were quite disagreeable places. The early convicts mostly were mutinous soldiers, murderers and rapists later joined by the political prisoners in after 1900s. There were less number of females for a large number of males leading to frustration, aggression, uneasiness, rape, murder and unnatural sexes. A well recorded case of Hina opened many facets of the British rulers in the islands. A boat with British sailors went to an Andamanese (Aka- bea) camp on instructions of the Col. i/c of the islands, Tytler with the purpose to establish friendship with the natives but one Mr. Pratt attempted to rape a Great Andamanese woman namely Hina (Topsy). At the moment her husband (Jumbo) with some fellow members killed Mr. Pratt with their arrows. Tura was later arrested for the murder. Hina was brought to the Ross Island the Officer-in-Charge of the Andamanese, British Clergyman Corbyn, where she learnt little English and sewing. Hina became very popular among the Britishers and the Andamanese as guide and interpreter. Later Corbyn took Hina and her Husband to Calcutta (present Kolkata) with an Andamanese namely Jacko with few children. Hina and Tura died in 1864 and 1882 respectively. There was another Andamanese lady with dubious background namely Ruth. She worked as domestic servant in the house of Mr. Homfray. She worked for some period in the Aberdeen School too.

In 1949, the forest department of the Andamans settled the Great Andamanese in Bluff Island. But their movement continued to be towards Port Blair where few the Great Andamanese occasionally were inhabiting the dilapidated Japanese bunkers (till 1976-77) and few were surviving on Tarmugli Island.

In 1969 the Andaman and Nicobar Administration settled the wandering Andamanese in a small island called 'Strait Island'.

A social worker from Bharatiya Adim Jati Sevak Sangh (BAJSS) was posted there to took after the aboriginals. Presently there is no staff from BAJSS on this island, but from Andaman Adim Janjati Vikas Samiti (AAJVS) since its formation in March 1976 and other departments and directorates of local administration.

Earlier there were separate groups of the Great Andamanese distinguished by separate localities, dialects and names. The territorial indigenous divisions of these tribes at that time, is given below.

Territorial Indigenous Divisions of Tribes

Sl. No.	Sub-tribe	Territory
1	Jeru	Southern part of North Andaman (particularly the present Kalighat area of Diglipur)
2	Kari	North part of North Andaman including present diglipur up to Landfall Island
3	Kora	East past of North Andaman
4	Bo or tabo	West part of North Andaman
5	Bea	West coast of South Andaman, Rut Land Island and Tarmugli Island.
6	Balawa	Neil, Havelock, Wilson etc.
7	Keda	Southern part of Middle Andaman
8	Kol	Guiter Island, long Island and eastern part of Middle Andaman.
9	Juwai	West part of Middle Andaman
10	Puckiwar	North Passage Island, Colebrooke Island, some parts of Baratang Island and Strait Island.

Assisting source: Chakravarty, D.K (1990).

Indigenously the Andamanese aborigines had limited territory. Members of one group were almost unaware of the detail of the neighbouring group. If a member of one tribe found himself accidentally adrift in his canoe, reaching the beach of another tribe he would be killed. Most borders between the territories were fixed and one tribe need permission to enter the other region. All the territorial bands can broadly be divided into two viz. Aryoto (shore dwellers) and Eremtaga (Forest dwellers). The Andamanese tribal groups inhabited the Andaman Islands from north to south are Kari, Kora, Bo or Tabo, Jeru, Kede, Juwai, Kol, Puckiwar, Balawa and Bea.

Interestingly the neighbouring languages stands more closest comparing to that of a distantly located tribal band.

Remarkably now the Great Andamanese are resettled at Strait Island which was indigenous territory of Puckiwar band but unfortunately no member of this band is alive.

It is informed by the Great Andamanese that a band called 'Shaari' is also existing among them. Jirake, Peje, and their blood relatives are members of this band at present.

During and prior to British period the Andamanese were having territorial divisions but colonization in the islands has affected them adversely and after 1969 when they were resettled in Strait Island, the territorial divisions and divisional restrictions have been abolished completely. Presently many of the above bands are no more and mainly Jeru, Kora and Cari and Bo are surviving.

The Andamanese do not build huts of a permanent nature. The communal hut of Great Andamanese is almost round. The roof is thatched with varieties of cane leave, dry leaves and comes down to the ground which becomes also the wall of hut. The hut is supported by the wooden or bamboo piles from inside. The communal hut is simply consisted of a large number of sleeping platforms and a fire place. The temporary or semi-permanent shelter consists of a sloping thatched roof under which there is a fire place and small sleeping platform. Apart from their traditional learning of construction of hut they also learnt methods of construction from the Burmese and labourers of forest department. Traditionally the Great Andamanese hut provides ventilation also. After the Great Andamanese were resettled at Strait Island by AAJVS and wooden houses constructed on the island for them, the aborigines gradually stopped making traditional hut and started living in the wooden houses. It was of course an appropriate step taken by the AAJVS in the contemporary circumstances.

The Great Andamanese are indigenously non-vegetarian. Their staple food consists of fish, pig, crab, dugong, shellfish, turtle egg, and tubers etc.

Presently, deer is not found easily in the island. The tribals as observed wait for a deer in appropriate season to hunt who often come to the island by swimming from opposite Islands. The eggs of birds are also collected to consume.

Staple Food of Andamanese

Sl. No.	Great Andamanese Name of food items	English equivalent
1.	Ra	Pork
2.	Oren	Deer
3.	Moche	Hen
4.	Chogbee/Toro	Turtle
5.	Tajiochor	Fish
6.	Ok	Prawn
7.	Ulukhu	Python
8.	Thumelonne	Honey
9.	Keyto	Crab
10.	Keftottcho	Banana
11.	Chulemo	Fruit (*Vimenia americana*)
12.	Kona	Fruit (*Garchinia* sp.)
13.	Chop	Fruit (*Termanalia procera*)
14	Tole	Diascoria
15.	Chaytaeera	Chilli

Contd. . .

Sl. No.	Great Andamanese Name of food items	English equivalent
16.	Toli	Potato
17.	Nyuri	Cat fish
18.	Carobolo	Variety of fish
19.	Pheno	Variety of fish
20.	Kharine	Variety of fish
21.	Tochol	Variety of fish
22.	Kwar	Variety of fish
23.	Jikar	Variety of fish
24.	Telebo	Variety of fish
25.	Karanj	Dugong
26.	Koeth	Variety of fruit
27.	Tomting	Variety of fruit
28.	Korbo	Variety of fruit
29.	Khider	Coconut

At present the Great Andamanese are free ration items on a prescribed scale by AAJVS as given in Table 4.

The Great Andamanese have well learnt the cooking method as in vogue in present non-tribal mainstream civilization of the islands. In order to consolidate the relationship of administration with the Great Andamanese the government representatives before independence used to supply them pigs and various food stuffs in exchange for various kinds of shells including turtle shells, resin and nest of hawabil (a kind of bird).

In kitchen garden the present Great Andamanese usually grow sweet potato, tapoica, chilli, papaya, pineapple, banana, guava, mango, lemon, some vegetables such as brinjal, okra, yam and sahajnafali etc.

Table 4 : The Free Monthly Ration Items distributed to the Great Andamanese and Onges

Sl. No.	Item	Quantity
1.	Rice	9 kg.
2.	Wheat Flour	5 kg.
3.	Sugar	500 gms.
4.	Pulse (Dal)	500gms.
5.	Turmeric powder (Haldi)	50 gms.
6.	Corriander powder (Dhania)	50 gms.
7.	Red Chilly powder	50 gms.
8.	Dalda	500 gms.
9.	Milk powder	500 gms.
10.	Tea leaves (BBT)	500 gms.
11.	Cooking oil	500 gms.
12.	Salt	500 gms.
13.	Kerosene oil	2 ltr.
14.	Bath soap	2 Nos.
15.	Washing soap	2 Nos.
16.	Match box	2 Nos.
17.	Candle packet (Per family)	1Pkt.
18.	Onion	500 gms.
19.	Tamarind	100 gms

The Great Andamanese are presently do not stay naked. Now women generally wear lungies and blouses but they are sometimes seen in either sarees with brassier and blouse or *salwar-kamiz*. Men wear shorts or lungies with vests and shirts but the young people full trousers with belt and shirts. The clothes periodically are distributed by the administration among the Great Andamanese. The indigenous dress of Great Andamanese is very simple. The men wear belts of bark fibre decorated with small shells while the women wear belts of pandanus leaves with some bark or leaves attached to it with the purpose to cover their breast. Painting the face was common in ancient period among the Great Andamanese. They decorate their bodies with zig-zag or other designs with clay paint specially tol-odu, a kind of white clay. In the turtle hunting festival young girls decorate their faces with clay.

The tribes of South Andaman cut their bodies with small flakes of quartz or glass in pattern of zig-zag or straight lines running up and down the body or limb. In the zig-zag design only two lines are made, the cut being incised at obtuse angels to each other and thus forming some thing like our "dog-tooth" pattern. The making of the pattern depends upon the individual test of the woman cutting them, but the face and ears, genitals, arms and knee pits are not cut.... Women are "Tattooed" in the same way as men. The non Andaman group of tribes have a different system of tattooing. The cut with them made by the men with the head of a pig arrow and are severe and deep.[13] But the tradition of making incision on body has been given up by the Great Andamanese and clay painting could be seen very rarely among them.

> "The marriage ceremony is simple and has nothing religious about it. As soon as the older of a tribe gets to know that a young couple interested in each other would like to get married, the bride-to-be is taken to a newly built hut. And there she sits while the bridegroom runs away into the jungle. After some seeming struggle and feigned hesitation he is persuaded to come back and made to sit in the bride's lap and that is it. They are now married. The marriage is strictly binding but, after death of either party other can remarry."[14]

Traditionally a marriage ceremony of the Great Andamanese has so many rituals that they go in a indigenous systematic way. At present the marriage ceremony among the Great Andamanese has been very brief and simple.

Few years back I received an opportunity to attend and witness a marriage ceremony among the Great Andamanese, here is the report—

Place	Strait Island
Date of marriage	14th January, 1997
Name of bride	Thong D/o Shri Peje
Name of bridegroom	Elephe S/o Shri Jirake
Age of bridegroom on this date	16 years, 25 days
Age of bride on this date	22years, 09months, 27days
Duration of ceremony	3 hrs. (1800 hrs. to 2100 hrs.)

In the courtyard of Shri Peje a pandal (big temporary shed) supported by bamboo poles and straitwoods 'khadiballi' was erected. It was decorated with frills of raw leaves of coconut trees. The supporting khadiballis were covered with wild leaves called 'paroto' in Great Andamanese language. Underneath the pandal a carpet of coconut leaves was laid; in front of which the sitting arrangements for the guest were made.

Two groups of women sat in front of the house of Jirake and Peje. They started singing folk songs based on their spirits, hunting and fishing games, the forest and the souls of ancestors etc.

Thirty minutes later the bride groom party led by Jirake arrived at the door of bride's house and pauses at the door for few minutes. At the moment women again started singing with clapping. On every turning on the way they did so. Finally they sat on the mat made of leaves under the pandal. All the officials (Field functionaries) including myself assembled at the place. We were requested by the King to take our places in front. The bridegroom was then made to sit on her lap on the mat. They remained for a few minutes in that embracing position. The pandal was completely electrified with the help of the official field functionaries so that the new pair and the ritual could be witnessed easily during dark hours. After this the then eldest person of the community Shri Nao (Sr.) came forward and gave preach to the new pair for a happy married life.

King Jirake, the father of Bridegroom came forward and shook hand with all of us and said thanks for coming. Now the arrangement for the folk dance was made. All the attendants assembled around the dancing ground, where at a corner the 'bomu' was placed. The bomu is a shield shaped musical instrument made of padauk (pterocarpas) by which a dance rhythm is provided by an Andamanese member by stamping it by his foot. The dance is called "Jurai" by the Andamanese.

The young members of both sexes came on the ground to dance together. They were ornamented with dentalium shells to produce clinking sounds while dancing. The Bomu was also found decorated with white clay by the women. The dancers started dancing together. But there was a restriction in the dance that every dancer had to dance on one foot on ground having the branches of "Paroto" in hands. The dance was with the rhythm produced by the Bomu beater. The dance ended after twenty minutes. When the dance was over we were called for the dinner. As marriage feasts *poori*, *kheer* with vegetables were served to us on banana leaves. The marriage ceremony thus ended with the dinner.

It was observed by the author that there was a wide change in the indigenous marriage ceremony of Great Andamanese with many addings. Earlier the resin torches were brought closer to the pair so that all present could witness the ceremony while in the ceremony attended the pandal was electrified and no resin torch was seen. Earlier the construction of pandal was not in practice. On the face of bride, the dots of white clay were made in a series starting from one end of eyebrow following the eyebrow line touching the forehead point (between both the eyebrows) ended at the end of the next eyebrow. This type of decoration is prevalent in the custom of a Hindu marriage. There was the complete absence of indigenous food items such as pork, flesh of turtle etc. and instead of it the Kheer (boiled rice with milk and sugar) and Poori (fried small *chapathi*) were served as marriage feasts.

Close consanguineous marriage is forbidden among the Great Andamanese but marriage with a distant cousin is allowed. Most importantly consent of elders is essential for marriage negotiations, though the girl's and boy's opinions are also considered important. The Great Andamanese do not wear any marriage symbol indigenously. Marriage is permitted for widows, widowers and divorcees. The practice of child adoption was once common among them but this is rare now for the reason of depopulation.

The Great Andamanese have retained some traditional customs in life cycle rituals. During the advanced stage of her pregnancy a woman is advised to sleep beside the hearth or open fire in the room. Before the delivery, a temporary hut is constructed beside the main hut. A fire is kept inside the hut to keep it warm. All the time of the delivery, only elderly females attend on the woman. After delivery, the mother is not allowed to do any work for about a fortnight. The child is given a name even before birth; as the nearest male relative or a friend of the family might request the couple to name their future child after him. In this way the Great Andamanese try to perpetuate their names.

On reaching adolescence, a youth is banned for some time from eating the flesh of a particular variety of turtle and some other foods. This ban is enforced only for a specific period and ends with a ceremony. Adolescent boys are called *Khilmil*. An adolescent girl is given a new name, usually that of a flower of the season.[15]

Their burial systems were somewhat quaint. A dead child is buried under the floor of the parental hut. The period of mourning after a death is three months. Indigenously the dead body of an elder generally tied in the tree was marked and festooned with cane leaves and for about three months no one visited the area. During the period of mourning which lasted about three months there was no dancing or any other festivity. At the end of it the remains of the corpse was taken down from the tree, the bones were washed, broken into sizeable pieces and used as ornaments. They were supposed to have therapeutic value also, as their mere touch could stop pain and cure disease. But now they generally do not shift out of their huts as they are constructed by the local administration with galvanized iron sheets and cemented floors.

Redcliff Brown (1948:109-10) mentioned two other funeral systems prevalent among these tribes viz. Sun Burial and

Cremation. The body was burnt only if anybody died on Warfare. Similarly the corpse of an enemy was burnt, from the belief that if the body was burnt so was the soul. The leader of the group who knew sorcery and witchcraft, and a also acted as medicine man was given the title of Akahchapan was given sun burial, a somewhat prestigious burial.

Recently the author witnessed a death ritual of the Great Andamanese. It was the dawn of the day of 21-08-2000, when we received a death news from Govt. G. B. Pant Hospital, Port Blair. The Senior Most member of the tribal community Shri Nao (Sr.) suddenly demised on the said day. We were shocked receiving this news. On the next day i.e. 22-8-2000 an official team consisting of the author as Consultant of AAJVS and Shri S. Barick from Anthropological Survey of India, Port Blair headed by Shri Som Naidu, Executive Secretary of AAJVS with the corpse in coffin and some Great Andamanese bereaved members reached the Strait Island by a boat namely MV. Kalpong.

When our team arrived at the jetty of Strait Island, the Great Andamanese members expressed their grief to us. The coffin was brought to the house of dead person. Right in front of the house there was an open fire. The tribal members brought the coffin into the house giving coffin a touch of the flame of fire with the indigenous belief that it would drive away the malevolent spirit if there is in the corpse. After a while the king of the community Shri Jarake sat down besides the coffin and started striking two shell halfs against each other which produced a jingling sound and in the rhythm of this sound the women started singing duet and solicited songs. During the singing a turtle hunting harpoon with rope was given touch to the coffin.

Some male members of the community went to the community graveyard selected a site to bury the corpse quite near to the grave of the dead man's first wife. When the male party after digging the grave returned to the settlement the female members immediately brought some straw typed extracts of plant called in their language 'Koro' and placed them right in front corners of the house. The age old tribal belief behind this practice was that as the dead person was a great hunter if he went out to hunt he could return with prey and not with the empty hands. The Koro serves success to the hunters and makes their return happy as per the tribal belief. All the children then paid tribute to the departed soul by planting burning incense sticks near to the coffin on the head side of corpse. The children were followed by the youths to do the same act. The clothes belonged to the dead persons were kept inside the coffin and the rest belongings such as tools, weapons, suitcase etc. were left in the grave with cuffing before closing the grave. All the presents including tribals and non-tribals stood near to the edge of grave and released handful of earth into the grave as a mark of paying of the last tribute to the departed soul.

After completely covering the grave all of us raised burning candles and incense sticks upon the closed grave.

The king Jirake with other followers stood near to the grave and prayed for a while for the departed soul to rest in peace. Thus, the recent death rituals of the oldest Great Andamanese ended.

Family is the only unit of social organization among the present day Great Andamanese. Earlier a group of families, consisting of 40 to 50 persons used to form a social division which Redcliff Brown called the "Local Group".[16]

In the past hunting, fishing and gathering were the economic activities among the Great Andamanese. The leader of the hunting and gathering group used to be addressed as *erjum*. The erjum is not a hereditary position but it was only the eldest man among the elders who was chosen for the position.

Earlier the division of labour among them was based on the strength required for the performance of various jobs. But the small size of their population at present does not favour such a system. In the past they had no notion of immovable and movable property included arrows, bows, various types of ornaments made of leaves, barks and shells.

A workshop to make and repair tools and weapons has been installed but no appropriate use was made by the Great Andamanese members. Their main implement has been now-a-days 'dah' a cutting implement. Earlier the tribes had learnt the use of iron which they often procured from wrecked ships on the sea shore. They made iron harpoons, arrow head made of iron, iron or wooden stick for digging, now they use a large varieties of tools and weapons used in the modern so-called civilized society.

Previously the Andamanese never caught fish with hook and line. As per the mentioning by E.H. Man, traditionally at low water the women and children with hand nets capture such fish and shell fish as are left by the receding waters in the rocky hollows on the foreshore, and at return of the tide the men are usually to be seen standing up to their waists in water, or pooling along the shore in their canoes and shooting with their bows and arrows at the fish as they dart past.

According to Man:

> "Canoes are made generally in the month of August and September and it takes about eight men nearly a fortnight to hollow out a canoe and form the prow. (The prow is for spearing fish and turtle). They generally select a tree trunk of anything between ten to thirty feet in length. First they remove the bark and then with an edge they shape the exterior of the canoe as also its prow. After that the interior is scooped out also with an adze. At the bottom level the canoes are about one and a half to three inches thick. They always use an outrigger, which helps maintain the balance.
>
> The outrigger is attached to a canoe by three or four pieces of wood, which pass through its interior. When alongside are shore the conoes are propelled by means of the haft of the harpoon spear which is used for catching fish when in deep water, paddles are used".

The religion of the Andamanese is according to Lieutenant Colonel Sir Richard Temple, who was Chief Commissioner of the islands and conducted the first ever general census in 1901:

"Simple animism (consists) of the evil spirit of the wood, the Sea diseases and ancestors and of avoidance of acts traditionally displeasing to them.

They have no rigid ceremonial nor do they believe in propitiation. But interestingly enough they do believe in an anthropomorphic deity called 'puluga' who according to Sir Richard again is the causes of all things "whom it is not however necessary to propitiate, though acts displeasing to him are to be avoided for fear of damage to the products of the jungle". [17]

The religion of the Andamanese is still partial animistic. The Great Andamanese believe in mythical beings like Biliku, Tarai, Puluga and Daria, the related legends and mythical powers controlling the natural forces and the Andamanese "Lau" is the name of an evil spirit. The Great Andamanese believe that their anger causes storm and rain. "Biliku" lives in a rock cave located in the English Island. In the past they would start collecting roots and fruits only after offering the first product of the year to Biliku, a practice that does not exist now. There is another spirit called '*Tharaye*' by the Great Andamanese.

As per the Great Andamanese belief, at the beginning, the earth was created and then the plants and the animals. Puluga (God) then created a man named Tomo. As instructed by God to Adam and Eve, similarly Puluga showed a particular garden to Tomo, the first man and told him not to eat the fruits of that garden which owned by Totachemi. Puluga also guided Tomo how to light fire by rubbing two pieces of Chom and Bel against each other. Before lighting fire Puluga asked Tomo to invoke Chana-Bi-Bhi (mother of son). As long as the fire burns, she stays there. Puluga sent his followers La-chi and Punga-au-bhola to Tomo to teach him the process of lighting fire and cooking pig's meat. Puluga created a woman to accompany 'Tomo' whose name was Chan-Aa-Ei-Labadie. Some present Great Andamanese old members say that she came to Bid Island and there she gave birth to several children. Tomo had two sons and two daughters.

The sons were Riola and Romila. It is Puluga who taught the Great Andamanese the art of making bow, arrow and canoe etc.

One band believes that Puluga lives with his wife in a big stone house in the sky. He is immortal. It is also believed that when the Great Andamanese were learning the things Puluga lived on Saddle Peak mountain. He gave the Andamanese their language the Puckiwar. The name of this tribe means "those who talk the original language" or they who speak the Andamanese language. It has been believed that (may be quite correct) that Puckiwar was closest to the native tongue. This legend reveals that the Great Andamanese are aware that they were once have a single language.

There is another evil spirit which is called 'Jirmu' by them. Instead of worshipping the spirits the Great Andamanese had practised some protective measures. They used to pray to their ancestors to do the needful to control the spirit and to protect them from any harm. Among the spirits, the Biliku is the main one. Strength of such belief is no more prevalent among the tribal youths presently.

Each tribe had contradictory versions to some extent and resembling versions to some extent in context of their myths and legends.

After the British occupation of the islands and when friendly relation was established with this tribe, efforts were made by Christian missionaries to convert those who were kept in the Andaman Home, but the efforts failed.

The Andamanese have lived mainly on fruits, tubers, fish, pork, dugong, crab, oyster, shellfish the eggs of turtles and sea gulls. But their contact with the outsiders, has brought a noticeable change in their food habits and manner of preparation.

In January 1997, the author joined the community members in the marriage ceremony of Ilephe and Thong. After the completion of all rituals and programmes as guest solemnly the author was served the wedding feast with special care. The feast items were completely as per the modern custom and cooking method.

The puri was served on a fresh banana leaf with a dish prepared of potatoes, cauliflowers, spices and oil. The 'Chatni', 'Salad' and little salt were placed at a corner of the leaf. After the author finished his meal the kheer (rice cooked with milk and sugar) was served and the taste was not strange to the author. He had enjoyed such taste in many Hindu marriages earlier.

It is very important to mention about a practice of adoption in common among the Great Andamanese.

Prior to British encroachment, the islanders had a marked system of reciprocal exchange. If a member of a neighbouring tribe should visit a friendly group that person could request an object of his or her liking and expect to receive it; eventually the receiver would be called on and the courtesy would be returned. Nowhere was the egalitarian nature of Andamanese society more pronounced than in their practice of adoption. In each of their ethnographic, E. H. Man (Superintendent of the Andamans from 1868 to 1871) and R. Brown dedicated much space to describe this practice. According to both authors, adoption occurred so often, it could be said that everyone was adopted. As Man said – "It is said to be of rare occurrence to find any child above six or seven years of age residing with its parents and this is because it is considered a compliment and also a mark of friendship for married man, after paying a visit; to ask his hosts to allow him to adopt one of their children".

Usually, the request was granted and the child left his own local group to live with his adopted parents. The new parents treated the adopted children as if they were their own, and the same was true for now the children treated their new parents. The children were not forgotten by their natural parents, who often visited or got permission from the adoptive parents to take the children with them for a time.

As part of their plan for the upliftment of the Andamanese, the British established an orphanage for Andamanese children. Children of all ages were taken in and "Civilized" receiving instruction in English, taught points on agriculture and Christianity.

Authorities hoped that those tribes which still remained hostile to the British would learn the kind treatment the children were receiving and be encouraged to establish friendly relations. The friendly relation the British had created with the Great Andamanese went beyond merely a political understanding. Apparently, the British became another tribe in the eye of the Andamanese, and as a result, the Andamanese extended to them the right to adopt their children. The British were unaware of the indigenous adoptional practice of the tribes when the orphanage first opened and as per the administrative reports at the time, they were surprised at how readily the islanders gave their children over to the British care. During the first year of operation (1869-70) the orphanage housed 37 Andamanese children, (15 girls and 22 boys) (Home/public1871-: 14-15). The Britishers wrongly assumed that the adult Andamanese realized the superiority of British civilization and were hoping to improve the lives of their children, totally being unaware of the indigenous trend of adoption in Great Andamanese.

At present the Great Andamanese are under all round care of an organization called AAJVS (Andaman Adim Janjati Vikas Samiti) situated at the capital Port Blair assisted by the Government. Their settlement has been electrified by solar plant and the DG set. The tribal students have been enrolled in the middle school at the Great Andamanese settlement and in some schools at the capital. The tribal members namely Nao (Jr.), Kaba, Bowa (Jr.), Loka, Meyo, Sullu, Gullet, Leechu and Noe have secured Govt. jobs in the different administrative sectors. Those adult members who are not in the govt. jobs are engaged by the AAJVS under the daily wages to clean and maintain their settlement and the plantations. Two old women are getting cash allowance from the AAJVS. A sub-centre to provide medical coverage to the tribes is functioning in their settlement. A society of their own namely 'Great Andamanese Multi Purpose Co-operative Society Ltd. ' is functioning to give economic protection and benefits to the tribes. Such development programmes have caused rapid change among the present Great Andamanese.

THE ONGES

The Onges, a negrito tribe are inhabiting the Little Andaman Island in Andaman District. The island has a geographical area of 731.5 sq. km is situated between 10° 30' and 10° 56' north latitude and 92° 28' and 92° 35' east longitude at a distance of about 100 km from the capital Port Blair.

The Little Andaman Island is almost flat and there is no mountain with no river. The presence of coral reefs around this island provides evidence of its emergence from the sea bed.

Prior to Mr. Portman's visit to the island it was completely isolated from the rest of the world. Portman became the first person to establish friendly relationship with the Onge, who were not allowing any outsiders to land and enter the interior part of the island. In historical period the Onge killed several intruders to stop intrusion into their territory.

The Onges were nomadic primitive people living in groups or bands in several parts of Little Andaman Island. The byres (Onge hut) were constructed both near the coast and in the interior of the island. Most of the Indian studies among the Onges have been conducted only after 1950s.

> "A rehabilitation scheme under the Special Area Development Programme initiated in the year 1964-65. There were about 249 Bangladeshi families, many families of Sri Lankan repartriates were also resettled here. In addition 169 Nicobari families were settled in Little Andaman. The relative proportion of the linguistic groups in terms of number of households and population gives us an idea about the population structure vis-à-vis the Onge population in Little Andaman Island. As per Taluk office Records from Hut Bay, Little Andaman, in 1987 there were 165 no. of Nicobarese households in Harminder Bay, 48 Bengali households in Netaji Nagar, 191 Bengali and Tamil households in Ram Krishna Pur, 246 families of Bengali, Tamil and Mopilah in Rabindra Nagar and Vivekananda Pur and 1755 households of Hindustani, Bengali, Tamil, Malayalam and Tribals from Chota Nagpur (Ranchi) in Hutbay settled

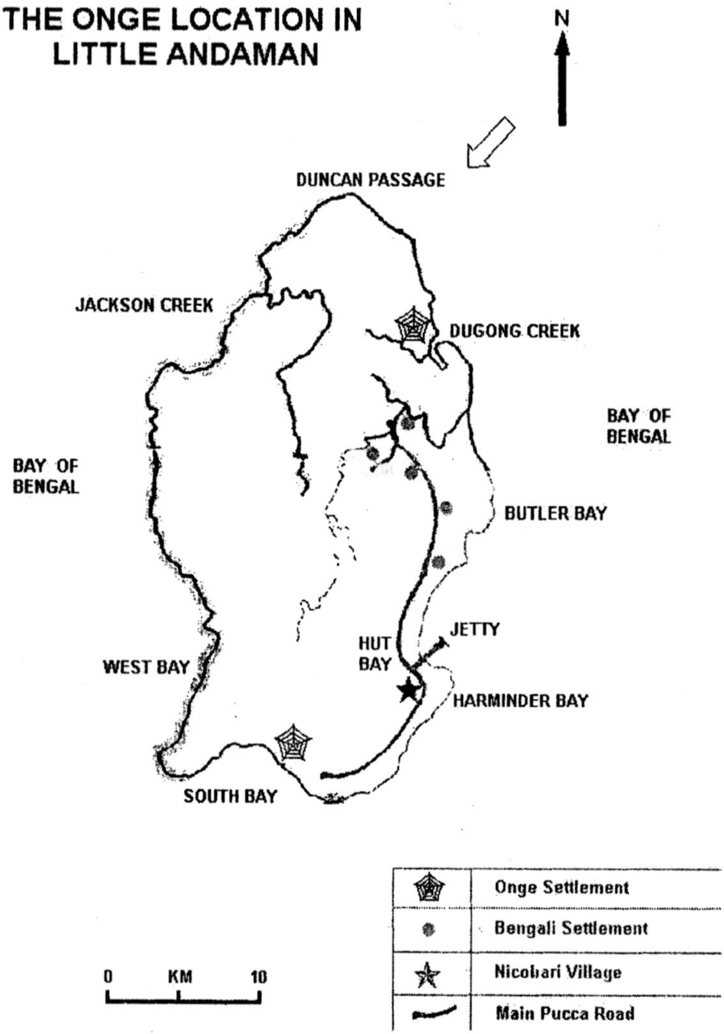
THE ONGE LOCATION IN LITTLE ANDAMAN
N
DUNCAN PASSAGE
JACKSON CREEK
DUGONG CREEK
BAY OF BENGAL
BAY OF BENGAL
BUTLER BAY
JETTY
HUT BAY
WEST BAY
HARMINDER BAY
SOUTH BAY
0 KM 10
Onge Settlement
Bengali Settlement
Nicobari Village
Main Pucca Road

on the island. During that period the non-Onge total population was 11,062 against the Onge population of 99 only."[18]

Presently the island has non-Onge population in five figures (above 13,500) against the population of Onge in only three figures (104).

Interestingly, Jarawas do not understand the word "Jarawa" because it is not derivatived from the Jarawa themselves similarly "Onge" word is not an Onge derivation. The Onges call themselves "Eniregale" which means 'absolute man.' But an intensive research is still needed in this regard to be carry out.

The Onges may be considered only one of their kind in the present world of negritos in terms of their complexion, short stature, presence of steatopygia (extra growth of buttock) among both the sexes, always being in happy mood. They have very less body hair on their parts. Their eyes are bright and big.

In a comparative study of the Onge with other tribes it was found out that the arch frequency of Onge is resembling with that of Asiatic Pygmies while the whorl and loops are similar to those of the Bushmen of Africa. In pattern intensity index oceanic Pygmies have higher average values than the African Negrittos or Negritos, Onge standing intermediate. The Onge steatopygia can be seen among the Bushmen of Africa. Much more details in this regard has been discussed earlier in this book.

The indigenous communal hut (Beyra) of the Onge was as a common residence for the members of a band.

The word 'gaiborale beyra' is composed of the Onge words, viz. gaiborale, i.e. forest and beyra i.e. hut, combining to mean 'forest hut' or a permanent type of hut in the forest. The hut appears like a huge umbrella or a bee hive. Its framework made of wooden poles and canes.

Among the Onges most cooking is done in the open except during the rains when the fire at the centre, which is larger than the fires by the sides is used. The concept of privacy is unknown; everything is open to every eye. The Onges were completely ignorant about the art of making fire that is why they always kept the fire burning, before matchbox was introduced to them.

The Onges are pure hunter-gatherers. They are not aware of agriculture. That they are an ancient people is evident, as already indicated from the presence of calcified shells at the base of their kitchen- middens. The Onge eat mostly natural food in which the island abounds. They are very fond of Jackfruit, Yam, Pandanus etc. The leaves of Pandanus sometimes provide roofing for Onge shelters. They particularly like pilchards. They generally harpoon the fish or shot with a bow and arrow. They catch molluscs, Crustacea, lobsters, crayfish and crabs even some kinds of hermit crab. They eat cicada too. They collect the pupae which are supposed to be a great Treat.

It is noteworthy that in the indigenous diet items of the Onge menu—birds, crocodiles, lizards, Jungle cats, bats, rats and snakes are not included because they harbour spirits of dead or malevolent spirits, as per Onge belief.

Apart from the receiving of free ration items on a prescribed scale monthly being supplied by the Andaman Adim Janajati Vikas Samiti, Port Blair, the Onge still go to hunt, fish and collect the forest and sea produces. The hunting, fishing and gathering are primitive Onge economy through which they receive their traditional food items/resources.

There are varieties of fish that are caught by the Onges with the help of their indigenous bows and arrows. Sardine, Barcuda, Seapearches, Shellfish, Horse Mackerel, Mackerel, Tunny, Mullet, Sylver Belly, Garfish, Shark and Rays, Prawns, Beaked fish Pomfrets carnex, Catfish, Hilsa, other parches and miscellaneous.

For easy and better understanding let us take a look at the diet items of indigenous Onge menu (Table 5).

In addition to the above mentioned diet items, the Onges have started consuming the free ration items that are supplied monthly by the Andaman Adim Janajati Vikas Samiti, Port Blair on a prescribed scale as provisioned for the Great Andamanese (see Table 4.).

Table 5 : Major edible items among the Onges

Sl. No.	Item	Onge Name
1.	Wild Pig	Ku
2.	Turtle	Naralange
3.	Turtle egg	Not Known
4.	Fish	Choge
5.	Dugong	Not Known
6.	Crab	Karkandu
7.	Honey	Taja
8.	Coconut	Nerchur
9.	Prawn	Ya
10.	Shellfish	Oage
11.	Wild fruit	Tibilachu
12.	Wild Potato	Digi
13.	Wild Nut	Dambera
14.	Wild Jackfruit	Bulundange
15.	Banana	Not Known
16.	Papaya	Not Known
17.	Roots & Tubers	Titakoru
18.	Roots & Tubers	Tebogeta
19.	Roots & Tubers	Gine
20.	Roots & Tubers	Tojokeage
21.	Roots & Tubers	Candalue
22.	Roots & Tubers	Toredalu
23.	Roots & Tubers	Gege
24.	Fruit	Chandalu
25.	Fruit	Naragero
26.	Fruit	Tejanya
27.	Fruit	Totketa
28.	Fruit	Marale
29.	Fruit	Gine
30.	Fruit	Dungjeco
31.	Fruit	Baloto
32.	Fruit	Jungene
33.	Fruit	Tejapto
34.	Fruit	Tekwakaco

The Onges have well learnt the method of preparing food from the non-Onge communities. Besides the new and indigenous diet items the Onge have started to consume betel leaf, betelnut, tobacco and deplorably some started intoxication of alcohol; however the bringing of liquor or any type of drug in Onge settlement by any outsider has been declared illegal and punishable under law. In this regard the Onges of Dugong Creek are much under safety while the South Bay Onge comes in the contact with a neighbouring Nicobari Community of Harminder Bay and in contact sometimes the Onge members receive toddy (Coconut beer) from the Nicobarese under non-official barter system.

The Onges were mother naked earlier, besides the presence of loin, nylon and cotton clothes among them, the Onge still had no proper concept of dress to cover the body for protection. The women have traditionally used the indigenous '*nakinyage*' a tassel made of tender palm leaves to cover their genitals. After they came in contact with the outsiders, they adopted the habit of wearing modern clothes to some extent. Now, the Onge males started wearing colourful shirts, trousers, vests etc. and females wear *lungies*, blouse, maxis, and skirts (young girls) etc. The Onge women still do not go for under garments.

They were thought to have a very special relationship with their spiritual world. The female genitals were believed to be that place wherein the power making the spirits of the dead dangerously dwell.

The crab, the flesh of which the Onges enjoy eating, also provides them with their roughly made and also obviously very ancient, smoking pipes. They use the claw, which is cut across the joint with a hole bored at one end to smoke aromatic leaves.

The Onges do not tattoo themselves, but use clay mixed with water to smear their entire bodies and draw patterns either with it or with red ochre mixed with turtle or pig's fat. The traditional practice of painting the body and face is still present among the Onges. It is a special job of women. The red ochre or white clay which is commonly used in painting is called '*alame*' by the

Onge. The necklace of dentalium or tusk shell is an important traditional ornament of the Onge women. On ceremonial occasion both men and women wear round their waist the traditional apparel *'Keye'* made with strip of cane and coloured bark fibre. The head band called '*ataki*' is also worn by both the sexes.

During the adulthood ceremony both boys and girls wear bark strips interwoven with bright yellow sheath of the dendrobium plant in a criss-cross fashion on the chest and the back and neckless and garlands of beads round the neck, arm and wrist.

The Onges now use wrist watches, shoes, sunglasses, sleepers, wrist bands and caps, etc., which is of course an outcome of the Onge-non-Onge contact.

Till the early fifties the Onges were living in several bands spread over the whole of the Little Andaman Island, comprised of few families. When an Onge is asked to refer to his or her communal hut, he or she will give a specific name. Each individual has been found to refer to one such name. The number of persons affiliated to one such name will vary from case to case. These names are nothing but the communal hut groups from which the living members claim descent.[20]

Bands are patrilineal, i.e. the members are descended through the male line only resulting in a group of agnates. Previously, pottery was existed among the Onges, which is evident from the findings of the kitchen-midden deposit. The pottery remains that found in kitchen-middens show the careful working of clay and could perhaps be as old as five thousand years. Presently, the art of pottery can not be seen among the Onges. Any pot is locally called *'buchu'* but the indigenous earthen cooking pot we discussed about is called '*tobochue*'. B.K. Basu (1990) writes:

> "I was fortunate enough to be able to get the only original cooking pot of the Onge collected so far by anybody. An elderly Onge named Dagulei helped me collect it from the dilapidated site of the communal hut of the "*Ingotijalo*" band at South Bay in Little Andaman.... The pots used to be made by coiling long and thin clay rolls and shaping them with the

controlled pressure of thumb and first finger. The pots were first dried in the sun and then baked. The potsherds collected from different places in Little Andaman are thicker, rougher, cruder and plainer, without any decoration, compared to those found at Chouldari in South Andaman".

The making of canoe is an important event in Onge life. The tree selected for canoe making belong to invariably to one of the species of Sterculia. It is first felled and then hollowed out with the help of simple hatchet. The Onges pay a great deal of attention when making the outrigger or the float along with the canoe because its object is to prevent the canoe from capsizing. Launching the decorated canoe is a ceremonial function. The Float or Outrigger is made of either *Hibiscus tiliacus* or *Sterculia villosa.* At the time when the canoe first time going out to sea the Onge pray to the benevolent spirits to save their canoe from storm or any mishap.

The Onges earlier used to make trips with their canoes to fish and hunt as far north as Rutland Island over 60 km of the open sea. Such trips were possible only because of a number of small islands are placed conveniently like stepping stones on the way.

The Onges always keep with them their bows and arrows. The bows are fashioned from a living trunk of a large tree called *Mimusops littoralis* or *Pterocarpur dalbergoides* and the string from long thin stripes of a particular kind of bark which is twisted together. Different varieties of arrow are made by the Onges for hunting and fishing. For hunting they use detachable arrow head and shaft arrow with the object being not only to shoot the animal with it, but also to ensure that it does not escape into the thick jungle. The fishing arrow of the Onges is called *'Korange'*. The arrow head is made of a slender iron rods of not more than 4 cm, but the head of arrow is found very sharp edged.

The drums drifted by the sea current are picked up by the Onges from the sea-shore and used as vessels for boiling pork, turtle and dugong and storing.

Table 6: Some Onge indigenous Tools, Implements, Containers and Other Items

Sl. No.	Article	Onge Name	Main purpose/Activity
1.	Bow	Aa	Hunting & Fishing
2.	Bow	Tokaibera	Hunting & Fishing
3.	Arrow	Chenokwa	Pig Hunting
4.	Harpoon Arow	Tena	Pig Hunting
5.	Arrow	Korange	Fishing
6.	Harpoon	Kuye	Turtle hunting
7.	Hand Net	Chika	Fishing
8.	Digging Wood	-	Digging & Chiselling wood
9.	Chisel	Cherange tokabe	Miscellaneous
10.	Adze	Toinyage	Wood cutting
11.	Bamboowater container	Koborange	Containing water
12.	-do-	Kuduwa	Containing water
13.	Wooden bucket	Ookoo	Miscellaneous collection
14.	Cane basket	Tockchu	Miscellaneous collection
15.	Earthen cooking pot	Tobuchu	Cooking
16.	Outrigger Canoe	Dange	Hunting, fishing & navigation
17.	Wooden Bucket	Tolahe	Honey collection
18.	Leaf Container	Tuluge	Storing of commodities

At present the Onges have started using different types of steel and aluminium utensils and vessels to prepare their foods. The outer civilization has left a great impact on the Onge material culture. The Onges have began to use all sorts of tool, implement, container and other domestic items that are available in the local market of outer civilization.

Fishing lines and hooks have taken places of bow and arrow in use generally. After the British advent, the dog reached Little Andaman in 1887 and the Onges widely adopted this animal by 1920s.

Earlier the Onges used nautilus shell for drinking water. Otherwise they drank like animals lying flat on their stomach lowering their heads and putting their lips to the water. Another shell they used was that of Tridacna, a giant clam. They filled it up with water and used it as a mirror when painting themselves.

A ritual 'getenkare' commences between February and March. The Onge believe that the ritual alone ensures the pregnancy of a woman.

There is a strong indigenous concept among the Onges in the context of birth. A spirit called '*Onkobowkwe*' sends souls of unborn babies to the wombs of Onge woman through a certain way. As per Onge belief, *Onkobowkwe* lives in Honey comb and when an Onge woman take the honey in her diet, soul sent by the spirit enters into her womb which causes her pregnancy. In spite of their knowledge of conception through sexual intercourse they believe that a woman cannot conceive unless *Onkobowkwe* desires it. On the other hand a childless woman is believed to be the victim of the curse of *Onkobowkwe*. This makes the honey most important diet item among the Onges. Interestingly when a matured beehive is seen they climb up the trees without providing any protection to their bare bodies and here the nature has come to their rescue. There grow bushes of a plant called '*tonjoghe*' all over Little Andaman Island. All they have to do is to chew some of the leaves of *tonjoghe* and smear the pulp all over their bodies even in their hair. Some they spit at the bees. This provides to them complete protection from bee attack.

At an advanced stage of pregnancy an Onge woman goes through the ritual of the 'gotechele' or '*ghotachelai*' (Rao, 1960, Roy and Ganguli, 1961) when she is ritually offered some items of food (pork, turtle meat, etc.) by any man, woman or child. The food is offered repeatedly and each time the woman spits it out after chewing. The person who offers the food enters into a kind of ceremonial or putative relationship with the child to be born.

By ritually offering food to the pregnant woman the person becomes the '*gutarande*' or '*gutarange*' of the child, once it is born. The child on the other hand would become the '*galankare*' of the *gutarandi*. Except for the special significance of this relationship during the performance of the birth and death rituals of the persons involved in it nothing more could be learnt about it.[21]

For delivery of child a particular hut is chosen. The young unmarried girls are allowed to witness the child birth. Experienced Onge women as we call in our society '*dai*' come forward to assist the mother. '*Batage*' leaves are spread all over the body of mother and on the ground for the parturition of the child safely. After the baby is delivered the umbilical cord is cut with a sharp indigenous bamboo or cane knife. But now iron knife or new shaving blade is used for this purpose. The navel of the baby is fermented with palms warmed in the fire of burning resin and then the baby is gently cleaned with the soft leaves of the 'Tejomo' or '*Taikutu*' tree. The placenta is buried in the ground around. The mother after the delivery and disposal of placenta is asked to sit on the bed of dry, warmed leaves. The belly of the mother is comfortably tied with bark strips of the '*Taibotilebe*' or '*Tej*' tree to bring back the uterus and abdomen into the normal state. For a certain period she is strictly restricted to consume meats and other edible items as directed by the elder members of the community.

The discussion on Onge ritual is incomplete if the "*tanagiru*" ritual is not mentioned. The end of the journey of an Onge member from adolescence to adulthood of life is marked by performance of a ritual called "*tanagiru*". Generally when a boy reaches at the age of 14 or 15 or 16 years he has to go through this ritual.

In the "*tanagiru*" the boy must go to forest and return with wild boar with his party, but path of coming must be different the way he went. After his coming with prey he is priorly asked to enter the communal hut not through the main entrance but a back opening. The elder brother or brother-in-law of the boy helped him to sit on the belly of the pig inside the hut. The boy as per ritual will not talk to anybody. He then drinks the clotted blood of the pig frequently. After the boy took ceremonial bath in the sea the boy's brother-in-law or elder brother cut the hunted pig into certain pieces and share among themselves. The day after, the boy is indigenously adorned and decorated by his sister-in-law or substitute. Clay painting can also be seen on this occasion on the body of the boy. The boy is then carried to sea by the male members of the community and he is made dipped thrice in the waist level sea water by the brother-in-law and others. Then his clay painted face is washed by his brother-in-law. Now he has to come out to the shore line where on sand some wooden logs of less than a meter in length separately kept straightly in a row. Each log has a certain distance from another. The boy has to cross carefully these logs one by one without giving touch to any log with his feet. Again the boy is decorated particularly by his sister-in-law (elder brother's wife). He enters the communal hut not through the main entrance but other opening. While entering the hut his hands should be stored on his chest. The end of the '*Tanagiru*' is not actually here at this point. He has to kill total twenty female pigs (some Onge said it 18-19 female pigs) to reach complete adulthood as per the ritual. After the killing of the prescribed number of wild boars again some ritual parts the boy has to go through. The boy, his elder brother or brother-in-law and his sister-in-law or substitutes have some dietary restrictions during the '*tanagiru*' ceremony. This is a very brief mention of the '*tanagiru*' ceremony which generally goes for more than ten days, and during these days several micro parts of the ritual are performed and which are still unresearched. It is another interesting fact that previously the Tanagiru was performed on many married Onge youths on different occasions. Thus it can not be said that this ritual is restricted to any martial status.

When a girl attains puberty the Onges perform certain rites and rituals. Redcliff Brown, author of "*Andaman Islands - A Social Study*" (1922), described it in these words:

> "On the occurrence of the first menstrual discharge the girl tells her parents, who weep over her. She must then go and bathe in the sea for an hour or two by herself. After that she goes back to her parents' hut or to a special shelter put up for the occasion. She is not required to go away from

the camp. All ornaments are removed from her, only a single belt of Pandanus leaf is attached round her waist, with an apron of cainyo leaves. Stripes of Pandanus leaf are attached round her arms near the shoulder and round her wrists, and others are placed as bands crossing her chest from shoulder to the waist on the opposite side, and crossing her abdomen from the iliac crest on the side to the trochanter on the other. These are so attached that the long loose ends hang down at the girl side. Bunches of leaves, either celmo or if these be not available, poramo are fastened beneath her belt before and behind. Other leaves of the same kind are placed for her to sit upon. Thus covered with leaves the girl must sit in the hut allotted to her, with her legs doubled up beneath her and her arms folded. A piece of wood or bamboo is placed at her back for her to lean against, as she may not lie down. If she is cramped she may stretch one of her legs or one of her arms, but not both legs or both arms at the same time. To feed herself she may release one of her hands, but she must not take up the food with her fingers; a skewer of cainyo wood is given her with which to feed herself. She may not speak or sleep for 24 hours. Her wants are attended to by her parents or her friends who sit near her to keep her from falling asleep. The girl sits thus for those days. Early every morning she leaves the hut to bathe for an hour in the sea. At the end of those days she resumes her life in the village. For a month following, she must bathe in the sea every morning at dawn."

To mark the first menstrual discharge of a girl, the rite of puberty is called '*Tamleangabe*'. Another description about this ritual is made by Basu, B. K. (1990). He writes, "At the first sign of menses, the girl puts some '*Batage*' leaves soft and soothing under her tassel and on the bed as well. As a part of the ritual, she abstains from eating any meat but can take fish, crab, honey, roots and tubers during the period, while the face of the girl is always kept daubed with white clay paste. At the end of the menstrual period the girl is led to the sea for a bath by few women."

The Onges are monogamous and divorce does not exist among them. Like other Negritos once they are married sexual fidelity is the accepted mode. But of course, before marriage, the young mix freely and no exception is taken to promiscuity. When it comes to the question of marriage, it can only take place with the consent of the family. Sometimes bride stays with her own parents after her marriage because of her small age. For instance, Miss Lilly, daughter of Bada Raju was married girl. She was married to Shri Prakash of South Bay. She was not allowed to go and stay with her husband till she possessed adulthood.

In 1911 M.C.C. Bonning, then Census Superintendent described about an Onge marriage as under. "Observed here for the first time an Onge youth with one hand and the hand of a girl of about 12 with the other hand. He then placed the hand of the suitor around the wrist of the girl and thus the young man carried her off never leaving hold to her.. This marriage took place on the shore and not a word was spoken at it. . . . I told him to let go his girl she ran away into the jungle as fast as she could and he had to leave her behind. (Census of India 1911:27-29).

Cipriani in 1953 reported that marriage accomplished in the communal hut of the bride. Here a bed is prepared in advance for the bridegroom, and on the nuptial day he goes to stop in it. During the night and while resin torches are kept burning giving good light, the bridegroom goes towards the bed of the bride, takes her by hands and brings her to his bed, where the consummation takes place, after which they sleep together for the night. This is done in presence of all the inmates of the bride's hut and is regarded enough. Sometimes ceremony is arranged by the parents without even consulting the girl. When this happens and the girl does not like him to be her husband instead of refusing him she hides herself in jungle.

At present the Onges do not necessarily follow the band or clan restriction in selection of life partner. When I asked Shri Totote, an Onge unmarried youth why did not he get married, he said that there was no matured unmarried girl among them (not among the same band/group members). After I asked to him "*suppose there is a suitable girl band out of your band, can you marry her now?*" He said – "*yes! Why not?*" It is apparent that the Onge to some extent have compromised with the chronological changes and the present situation. Cross-cousin marriage is preferred by the Onges. Remarriage of widow and widower is also prevailed among the Onges.

From the excavation of kitchen-midden pot sherds have been found which date back more than 2000 years. With the passage of time the artistic expression of the Onge through pottery has gone of the Onge mind.

Among the Onges, infants quite often are headloads of mothers hanged with help of bark slings, while the fathers make toy bows and arrows for the walking children to learn the game of hunting and fishing. Adoption of children has been quite frequent which express their great love and care for their children. A couple can give away their child to another community on their own discretion.

Among the Onges after death, the corpse is buried under the bed of the deceased person, generally in the temporary hut. The married *gallankare* or *gutarandi* or any substitute of the deceased mainly performs the rituals particularly in disposal of the corpse. The grave place is selected under the bed of the dead person. The dead body is positioned with folded knees, eyes covered with palm leaves then tied with '*kuebc*' strips. Licuala palm which is called '*Tumeroe*' in Onge are thrown over the corpse in the grave before closing it with earth. After months they dig up again the grave to receive the lower jaw of skeleton of the dead. A mandible is made with this jaw part and worn around the neck. It rotates from one relative to another after few days. The duration of death mourning completes with a communal dance by the male and female members. In dancing the Onges have no accompaniment, not even the sounding board like that of the Great Andamanese-. Both men and women participate. They go round and round holding each other's hands and while they dance, they sing.

When an Onge was asked why they bury the dead underneath the bed of the dead. Simply he told that the spirit of the deceased after such practice live with them to protect and help them.

The Onges have no clear concept of religion but they are animistic. They do not believe in sacrifice or propitiation. The Onges have their own legends. As per Akar-Bale belief, in the very beginning there was no night or darkness then one of their ancestors crushed a cicada and the cry of the insect brought darkness upon the world. However, the souls of the ancestors are believed to be the tutelary spirits for them.

As per an Onge tale, they migrated out of Kalapahad because some supernatural power did not want them to stay there. After passing a long distance they reached a place called '*Tambegey*' and they did not stay there and moved further. Further they reached a beautiful place called *'Tokobuley'* which is now known as "Dugong Creek". They started living at this place.

One day to visit their old place 'Kalapahad' of South Andaman they made canoes with hard labour. When they reached amidst the way severe storm arose and as result many of their members lost their lives and several canoes destroyed. It was the anger of the evil spirit '*Tomale*'. The escaped members began to worship *Toya-bog-lanko*, the great supernatural power and the storm subsided. The sea became calm and the members returned back safely.

Before their resettlement at Dugong Creek and South Bay of Little Andaman Island by the AAJVS Onges were dispersed. Before the island came into the effect of the settlement scheme; almost all portions of Little Andaman were occupied by the Onges. Some of the communal huts were Tuagalangae, Nachugae, Uide, Oubaitai, Tulai, Chemalai and Badegai, etc. Their movement to hunt and fish with their indigenous canoes between Little Andaman and Rutland Island was quite regular but with their resettlement with introduction of monthly free ration by the AAJVS made their such moves rare.

A family is the constituent unit of the band. The Onge band today is no more a corporate unit in the true sense, the families are also not very strongly organized. In course of my staying and investigation amidst the Onges of Dugong Creek, a case has come out to my notice. In the case a widow namely Sheela birthed a child while nobody dared even the *'raja'* (King) too, to ask her about the actual father of the child. The widow lost her husband years ago. It was observed that the concept of the 'right to seniors' and the subordinate of juniors is unknown to the Onge. The concept and status of "Raja" has been introduced recently by the AAJVS in the interest of better administrative control over the Onges.

However within all the given circumstantial limitation, bands among the Onges have been considered as social groups having some common mutual obligation towards each other, the members of which have certain obligations or modes of affiliation to their respective bands.

Now the Andaman and Nicobar Administration have all round control over the Onges community. Some are engaged in the wage labour and some have been appointed in the administrative sectors. Monthly free ration on the prescribed scale have been provided to them by the AAJVS which promoted the Onges to be idlers to a larger extent. Going into the sea and forest for hunting and fishing activities have been not so essential part of their traditional subsistence economy. Apparently the friendship with outsiders of the Onges has proved to be too expensive for them and the British diplomacy deserves much of the credit.

THE JARAWAS

The Jarawa are one of the Negroid tribes of Andamans. The word "Jarawa" is derived from the Great Andamanese language which means 'stranger' in Aka bea language, while the Jeru band call the Jarawa as 'Kontoka' which means 'the man who shoot arrow'. The Jarawas name themselves as *"Aang"*.

The ferocious tribe, Jarawas had been fighting the neighbouring Aka-bea for centuries till the British made their advent to stay in

1858. The Aka-bea, the British, the escaped Indian convicts, the Japanese or the pirates whoever came the belligerent Jarawa fought against them. Their xenophobia ended in 1998.

Radcliff Brown (1948) is of the opinion that 'they are the descendants of emigrants who at some time in the past made their way across from Little Andaman and thrust themselves in upon the inhabitants of Rutland Island and the South Andaman maintaining their footing in the new country by force of arm.

In the previous documents and reports the inhabitants of North Sentinel Island were also addressed as 'Jarawa' who now are known as Sentinelese.

The Jarawa tribes territorially have been limited to the westcoast and region of South Andaman and Middle Andaman Islands. An area of about 649 sq. km. has been notified as "Jarawa Reserve " under the A&N Islands (Protection of Aboriginal Tribes) Regulation 1956.

"The first recorded reference to the Jarawa is contained in a journal kept by Lt. Robert Hyde Colebrook (who was to end his career in India as Surveyor General). He made a voyage around the Andaman in 1789-90, in the company in Commodore (Later Sir) William Cornwallis, brother of the then Governor-General of India, Lord Cornwallis. In an entry dated 26th December, 1789 he writes about going up the harbour in Port Cornwallis (now Port Blair). When they went ashore to look at a hut which appeared to be inhabited."

They found it deserted. He wrote:

It was a most wretched little shed, built of sticks and leaves. We found in it some bones, which appeared to be those of a wild hog, suspended to the roof by strings. The ground about the hut was strewed with the shells of oysters, mussels, cockles, and other shell fish. In returning down the creek, we discovered one of the natives in a tree. The instance he perceived us he ran down with as much agility as a monkey, making a great noise and calling to two others who were

> below. One of them we took to be a woman, by her voice as we could not see her.

In a subsequent monograph published in the *Journal of the Asiatic Society of Bengal* in 1794, Colebrook again writes about the aborigines, he encountered during this particular voyage:

> "They go quite naked the women wearing only at times a kind of tassel or fringe round the middle; which is intended merely for ornament, as they do not betray any signs of bashfulness when seen without it".

Those who have seen the Jarawas in recent years will find a ring of authenticity in this description. Besides, in the specimen vocabulary of the Andamanese language that Colebrook had compiled and which he published in his monograph Portman found that nearly half the words he had picked up belonged to the language of the Jarawas."[22]

In 1790 Colebrook closely saw few tribes plying a canoe near the present Dandaspoint. Some of their words collected by him were found to be of the Jarawa language. This leads to the inference that the Jarawa had canoes about 200 years ago. But when the second penal settlement was established in 1858 no Jarawa could be found near the harbour area. The entire harbour and the areas around the settlement were completely occupied by the Great Andamanese tribes.

Another report informed that the Jarawa had canoes:

> "On 16th November, 1884 Portman's expedition enchored near to the Cinque Island when they saw some smoke coming out of the jungle. Three canoes of the Jarawas found there, were kept on board. Oldham, the incharge of operation captured and brought nine of them to Port Blair and after a long stay they were taken back and made free."[23]

Due to some unknown reasons the Great Andamanese were much stronger tribes by the time of the second settlement. They occupied the entire areas around the harbour and the Jarawa were driven into the hinterland. There were several skirmishes took place between the two groups. Some major battles fought between them are unrecorded but firmly can be guessed by us.

Supported by the Great Andamanese there were many attempts made by the Britishers to capture the Jarawa and bring them under the British influence. On some occasions Jarawa members were captured and kept under captivation for few days with suppose to befriend the Jarawas could not be achieved. The Jarawas under captivation either died of sickness or became so unhealthy that they had to be released by the rulers.

But during the second penal settlement when efforts were made to establish contact with them they were found to be much more hostile. How and why their friendly disposition of 1790 turned hostile over a span of 70 years or so requires scrutiny for proper understanding of the behaviour of the Jarawa.

One reason contributing to the continued hostility was the use of Aka-bea trackers by the British against them.

While speaking of the negritos of the Andamans as a whole, Grierson remarked that philologists have not yet succeeded in connecting them with any recognized family of speech. (Grierson, 1967). Nair collected some linguistic data on this tribe when two adult male Jarawas were brought to Port Blair, for about three weeks in January 1977. According to him,

> "This language has intense nasalisation and aspiration of stops. The presence of velar fricative and pharyngeal fricative is also a peculiar feature of the language." (Nair, 1979).

The studies at initial stage reveal that the sound system of the Jarawa language attests 13 vowel phonemes and 26 consonant phonemes. The word system of the language attests six words classes namely noun, pronoun, verb, adjective, adverb and particle (Rajasingh 2002:116-119).

The language of the Onges and the Jarawas structurally and lexically show more resemblance. The author has collected as many as 20 words from the Jarawa language that are resembled to the Onge words of same meanings. Some south Indian words can also be obtained from a Jarawa tongue such as Poitte, ni, ekadde, etc.

The Jarawas of the Middle Andaman live within the reserve forest area from Lakda Lungta to Chotalingbang Bay, stretching longitudinally over a distance of about 25 km. In South Andaman they inhabit the reserve forest starting from the Tirur area up to Spike Island along the west coast. Within the reserve forest we can see three types of settlements: Permanent, Semi-permanent and settlement used for a few months.

The Jarawas inhabit today the west portion of South Andamans and Middle Andamans. It has three social discernible territorial divisions viz. Northern group, Central and Southern Group. The northern group inhabit the Kadamtala adjacent areas called 'Tanmad', the southern group inhabit Tirur area called 'Boiab' and the central group inhabit the RK Nallah adjacent areas alongwith the ATR (Andaman Trunk Road) area called 'Thidong'.

The present Jarawa community bears a large portion in the population as reproductive active population of teenagers and young members. The marriage generally occurs between the adolescents. A widow/widower can get marry in the Jarawa community. Though the Jarawa are strictly monogamous, subsequent marriages are common. The children after six or seven years do not share the sleeping place with their parents but live with other children and move from one place to another independently till they get married.

D.L. Morgan in his description of an encounter with the Jarawas which took place on 26th February, 1918, mentioned the Jarawa village:

> "The village consisted of 10 huts inhabited by 20 to 30 Jarawas. Each hut was about 3 feet high and 6 feet square. The diameter of the village was about 20 yards. There was thick jungle on all sides, a small nallah running down one side. He said he had been able to destroy two communal huts, but does not specify whether there were any Jarawas inside the huts at the time of destruction. "

Morgan went on to report:

> "I came across over 20 old Jarawa villages. Each village had between 7-15 huts. The jungle is full of well beaten tracks. Each of the two communal huts which we destroyed was capable of holding 100 persons. There were several women and children in the village which we raided on the 28th of February. Wherever we found grown-up Jarawa footprints we also found footprints of their children. We recovered a large number of nets and small bows. The nets are made by the Jarawa women, and the small bows are used by the children. "

The Jarawas call their hut or settlement as Chadda, residence of a family as Tutime chadda and residence of unmarried boys with or without widower inmates as Thorkalang chadda and a maiden's residence with/without widow inmates as Thorkongo chadda.

A community hut wherein more than 20 Jarawas at a time live, can be easily seen on Andaman Trunk Road side near R.K. Nallah in South Andaman. This hut is bee-hive shaped constructed with thatched roof and has few supporting poles inside the hut. The semi-permanent huts can be seen at Foul Bay, Yadita area, Chhotalingbang Bay, Jullan Pather and Goal Tekrey etc.

A Jarawa hut or settlement is natively called '*Chadda*'. A lean-to-type temporary hut used by a couple with unmarried children is called '*Tutime chadda*'. A semi-permanent shelter is known as *Chadda de Thuma* or *Chadda de utthu.* The hut where a widow resides is called *Thorkalong Chadda* and maiden's or widow's dormitory is called *Thokotongo Chadda.* The roof of hut is called Wilpo which is thatched with cane leaves and palm leaves.

A permanent space is demarcated in the community hut for each family which is called Thule in Jarawa language. A hearth can be seen at a centre of the community hut above of which a platform to hang or keep pig fat and meat is made. There can be seen a number of pig and turtle skull in bunches hanging from the roof tied with cane strips.

When they hunt any pig in the forest immediately they bring out its intestinal parts through whole made by arrow on its stomach. Then they insert palm leaves inside the stomach. When it is ready to put on fire they remove the leaves out. The toes are detached from the body and the pig is made to sit on fire and after a while it is rolled on fire. The Jarawas of other areas usually come and join them in eating pork. After eating pork they use a tooth pick called '*Mahu*' by them.

The Jarawas are still at the primitive stage of life on earth. They entirely depend upon forest and sea for food. Wild boar (*Susscorfa andamanensis*) and monitor lizard (*Varanus salvator andamanensis*) are happily consumed but not deer ('*topiaali*' in Jarawa language) and bird ('*noha*' in Jarawa language). The deers are found in plenty in 'Jarawa reserve'. Various kinds of fruit and tubers too are parts of their diet. Many other forest produces which we are not aware of are used by the Jarawas in their food. Sea is the fishing ground for them and edible molluscs are also collected by them for their consumption. Trochus (*Trochus niloficus*), bivalves, turbo (*Turbo maramaratus*), rock oyster (*Saccostrea cucullata*) are boiled on fire before consumption. Crab, big and small lobsters are also boiled. The varieties of animals from the Jarawa dietary menu. These can be broadly divided into Mammal, Aves, Reptilia, Pisces, Mollusca, Crustacea and Insecta groups. Some of these groups are: Wild pig (*Susscorfa andamanensis*), Andaman Water Monitor (*Varanus salvator* andamanensis), Dugong or sea cow (Dugond dugon), Green Sea Turtle (*Chelonia mydas*), Olive Ridley Turtle (*Lepidochelys olivacea*), Giant Marine Cat Fish (*Arius thalassinus*), varities of fish, Mullets (*Liza melinoptera* and *Crenimugil crenilabis*, etc.), varieties of edible molluscs, spiny Lobster (*Panulirus versicolor*), prawns of different families and crabs of different families, etc. The skulls and shells of turtles and skulls of wild boars can be seen hanged in a Jarawa Hut. Honey and jackfruit are also very important foods of Jarawa. In the honey collection the Jarawa tie with the body some leaves of a plant called '*Uya*' to drive the bees (*Onyoma).*

The person who first locate a beehive in the forest gets the traditional right to collect it. If he cannot collect immediately when sighted a few shrubs around the tree on ground are broken to notify others that this beehive has already been located.

Traditionally food is cooked in pit ovens called '*aalaw*'. They boil the edible things in aluminium vessels called '*busu*' which are obtained from the AAJVS as gifts and the adjacent villages through raids.

The Jarawas consume cooked food and never raw to the extent that unriped fruits are boiled and eaten. The food items like pork or fish is put on the stone bed which is roasted by the direct fire as well as by hot stones.

The Jarawas of both sexes go complete naked. However some ornaments are worn by them but these are not in the sense to cover their nudity. A bark thick chest guard called *'Tohe'* is used by the adult male members when they go out to hunt. The adorning articles used by the Jarawa are head band, necklace, armlets and waist bands. These are mainly made of palm leaves and shells. The necklaces and the headbands of red thread which the administrative party gave during the contacts are also used by the Jarawas. The headband is called in Jarawa language '*aanotahe*' while armlet is called '*Oetahe*' in Jarawa language. They call their waist girdle as '*wayetahe*'.

With the increased contact with the outsiders the Jarawa began to use cloth items (kangapo). They began to make their ornaments from the thread of clothes in place of or added to the forest materials. The temporary ornaments are mostly named after the plants from which the materials are collected while the permanent ornaments are made of mainly shell, cotton thread and bark strips. The Jarawa of both sexes decorate their body and face with clay. After eating pig or monitor lizard they invariably smear their face and body with clay and make designs on it in which certain designs are common.

Their folk songs revolve around their material culture and hunting, fishing and gathering activities.

In course of may investigation among the villagers of the villages located near the Jarawa reserved forest and which are affected by the frequent Jarawa raids, I noted that for the villagers there are two divisions of Jarawa. First, the thief Jarawa of Middle Andaman who come and steal the things and foods of their needs from the non-tribal settlement at night and second, the cruel Jarawa of South Andaman who come and kill the settlers and their animals. But it may be added that now the Jarawas are not man killers. They have been befriended. From the study of the past Jarawa killings, it is assessed that most of such killings were as revenge taken by the Jarawa against the illegal activities and causing to disturb the peaceful life of the Jarawas by the outsiders.

The economic activities of the Jarawas goes around their traditional games of hunting, fishing and gathering from sea and forests.

The Jarawas are very good swimmers. They come across the creeks in the Jarawa area between South Andaman and Middle Andaman in course of their economic activity and in movement from one habitat to another. It is noteworthy that the Jarawas do not reside at a place permanently. It has been observed that the Jarawa of R.K. Nallah area visit Uttara area while the Jarawas of Dhani Nallah of Kadamtala visit Middle Strait. Their movement from one place to another place has one more reason and that is their kinship or friendship with other groups, but their economic purpose often becomes the basis.

There are specific divisions of labour among the Jarawas when they are on movement. Male members pick and carry their hunting implements and clean the way, the female members carry the food articles and other household belongings. On reaching the new site for camping purpose the ladies with children go to collect poles and leaves for making temporary hut/shelter and the men go for food collection. The maidens erect their own shelter and go out for food collection.

After the Jarawas have been befriended by the outsiders their movement through the ATR occupying tops of running buses and through other vehicles has become a normal scenario today. Thus their use of the traditional forest route is reduced.

In October, 2000 a group of Jarawas consisted of about 30 members came from Tirur area of South Andaman and constructed a community hut on ATR road side near Punnanallah area. This new habitat was called *"Tulichadda"* by the Jarawas. After they began to stay at this new habitat their friendly relationship with the neighbouring Jarawas of R.K. Nallah area has got deeper root. If any of both the groups killed one or more pig, then the other groups get invitation to come and join the hunter groups in eating pork. After eating the pork they smear red clay on their faces and body parts. The Jarawas believe that this practice protects them from disease of several sorts.

The Jarawa bow is called '*aao*' in their language which is made of chuiood (*Sageraca elliptica*) while their arrow is called 'Patho'. Their wooden head arrow is made of Arecca Wood (*Arecca trianda*). They use iron and areca wood or Bambo to make iron head arrow called *'aetaho'* in their language. One more iron head arrow is constructed by them which is called '*ochchale tahape*' in the native language and they use iron and chuiwood to construct it. Their harpoon arrow is called '*tahowai khoab*' which is constructed with the use of iron, cane and areca wood.

The arrow is generally called 'patho'. They have different types of arrow. They make iron arrow with help of chisel, hammer without tempering it on fire. So stone aged foragers they are. Their chest guard is called 'kekad' used by the adult male members during their hunting activities. They insert their knives called 'towa' in it.

'Towa' is most popular implement among the Jarawas which they use in cutting pork in pieces. It has a shape of an arrow with no stick but has a wide breadth of 4-6 inches. They keep *Towa* in their waist guard known as '*tohe*' in Jarawa Language. Their

iron edge tied with wooden handle is called '*toub*' by which they mainly make bow shape in wood.

During my stay in Jarawa hut of Punnanallah area I observed mainly two types of weapon viz. '*Thom*' and '*Thosulatetoha*'. '*Thom*' is a Jarawa word called for pointed iron arrow, which generally is found with the length of 4-5 inches. *Thosulatetotoha* is an iron arrow head while its supporting stick or shaft is called '*thene*' or '*thenang*' by the Jarawa. To sharpen the edge of their weapons and implements they use stone called '*Ulli*' in their language.

They use wood cane and iron to make their adze. Their digging stick of iron is called '*wohen*' while bucket of *taung peing* wood is called ' *uhuo*'. They call their basket '*taj*' to make which they use cane. They collect nylon nets from the sea shore and shallow water to make their small net bag to store their collected stuffs and mainly fish. They also construct their fishing hand net with bark, bamboo and cane and call it '*potochehut*'. Their indigenous knife made of stone is called '*ulihe*'. Their indigenous torch (*tuhu-ga*), is made with 'dhup' (*Canarium euphyllam*) and dhani leaves.

In the adolescent ceremony the boy has to hunt a wild pig and offer to his kin and others. The *Opemame* ceremony of girl is observed when she attains puberty. As per the custom they rename their children during /after the adolescent ceremony.

On the first menarche of life movement of the girl is restricted to a limited space bordered by four posts and she has to keep her eyes closed. A paste of red clay called alum, pig fat and gum from a creeper is applied on her head, neck and entire face. During this period she is restricted to speak. Certain restrictions she has to follow on food in which chiefly she cannot eat pig and honey. What she can take only are *Onog* (a variety of edible mollusc) and *Eeng* (water). After three days she takes bath and there after no restriction stands before her. All gather around her. She is then dressed with floral ornaments. The women and girls do sing and dance. As contraceptive leaves known as *Vachahi* and *Hatho* are used.

During first pregnancy the lady and her husband do not use any apparel or ornament and do not decorate their bodies with white clay. The lady does not accept anything from the non-Jarawas. During parturition the lady is given a separate corner. The umbilical cord is cut by sharp arrow head. The elderly ladies attend the child birth. On the new birth the happiness is expressed by clapping by the attending ladies while the grand mother of the newborn starts crying. After a while they sing and dance to celebrate the occasion. The fat of monitor lizard is used to massage the new born babies.

The Jarawa engrave geometric designs on their bow with iron knife, make intricate designs with lines on chest guard or wooden bucket and decorate the same with strips made of orchid stems.

The sun (*ehey*), moon (*taape*), sky (*pangne*), stars (*chilope*) and cloud (*ethibithi*) have their great role in the Jarawa myths and legends. The full moon is called '*utthutaape*' and small moon is called '*poniya taape*'. The high tide is called '*chakte*' while low tide is called '*chigia*'.

The Jarawa have certain traditional medicines and health practices such as to clean the genitals during the menstruation period abstract of *Dracaena angustifolia* Roxb species called '*Tidba*' in the Jarawa language. Bark and leaf coagulant of *Knema andamanica* called '*Oro*' is used. Against cough and fever the leaf and stem of Uiyaw (*Amomum aculeatum* Roxb) is tied around the chest while its juice is applied on scar. The leaves of *Chromolaena odorata* are used as coagulant on leech bite. The leaves of *Myristica andamanica* is used to stop bleeding and as garland when one is sick. The leaf wrapped around body against pain is called Intoto (*Piper betle* L.) (Piperceae). Against the throat infection the plant of Urubethe (*Trichosanthes bracteata* (Lamk) Voigt. (Cucurbitaceous) is wrapped around the throat.

For making huts the Jarawas use the following plants/plant part/tree/tree part mentioned by them. *Tulu* (*Areca triandra* Roxb.), *Keen* (*Baccaurea ramiflora* Lour), *Ottang* (*Calamus andamanica* kurz), *Totanahi* (*C. grandiz* kurz), *Tyele* (*C. pseudorivalis* Becc.), *Indau* (*Caryota mitis* Lour.), *Oro* (*Knema andamanica* (warb.) de Wilde, *Pepe* or *Popo* (*Licuala peltata* Roxb.) and *Thuiya* (*Nypa fruitcans* Wurmb.), etc.

They use the flowers as ornaments such as *Didu* (*Bombax insigne* wale), *Manguyanwe* (*Barringtonia ariatica* (L.) *Kurz* and *B. racemosa* (L.) spreng), Dema (*Acacia auriculiformis A. cunn.*), Hokatet (*Cerbera manghas* L.), Taon (*Dendrobium crumenatam* Sw.), *Leedau* (*Donax canaeformis* (Forst F.), *Weeseag* (*Fagraea racemosa* Jack. Ex. Wall.), *Oha* (*Ixora finlaysoniana* Wall. ex. G. Dau), etc. They use the fruit *Inetoha* (*Combretum latifolium* Bl.) in making garland besides some leaves are also used to adorn themselves.

Their Resin torch is a tied leaf stick filled with Resin powder (*Canarium euphyllum* kurz) called '*Phone*' is burnt while moving at night. When they are in the forest and no water source is found nearby, in such emergency they use stem juice called *Ottang* (*Calamus andamanicus* Kurz.). The Twig (*Pongamia pinnata* (L.) Pierre) called '*Aichum*' is used sometimes for cleaning teeth. To trap the pig they spread Twig (*Plecospermum andamanica* King) on the spot.

The Jarawa rituals pertaining to the birth, marriage and death are still unknown to the larger exent owing to their unfriendly attitude towards the outsiders till recently. On their death rites Jayanta Sarkar (1990) reports:

> "The term penchame is used by the Jarawa to allude to death. During our visit we did not come across any case of death. Thus the rites related to death remain unknown. Only once did we see the reaction of a few individuals after they received the news that the brother of one of those present had died.
>
> On 13th January, 1988, we took 55 Jawaras to the west coast near Tirur. Four Jarawas including a woman and a boy, swam across and came to our dinghy. Immediately after they reached the main boat, one of them conveyed the news of the death

of the brother of a man who was with us on the boat. He bagan to wail loudly. He laid down on the boat and continued to cry. Two women sitting nearby didnot say anything but kept their hands on his body as a sign of sharing in his grief.

The man who had brought the tidings of death, his female partner and the bereaved man came and sat at one place. They were joined by the female partner of the bereaved man. The four of them brought their heads close together and then, placing their hands on one another's back, began to cry. . . . In the afternoon, when we took 3 of the 4 persons of South Andaman ashore at Spike Island he came down with us, collected an unfinished bow and arrows which he had left there that morning as well as other things from a temporary hut, took off his chest guard and gave it to the man who had brought the death news. Even at this juncture he was not seen to talk.

After the death of a person, the small bones in the case of adults and lower jaw bones in the case of children are taken out. The Jarawas have been found to wear small lower jaw bones or clavical bones or other small bones of the deceased around the neck or around the waist. When asked they indicated that they were the bones of a deceased child or kinsman."

The Jarawas do not bury their dead, while Onges and Great Andamanese bury their dead. [25]

The Jarawas generally dispose of a dead inside the forest away from their camp. They leave it between the buttresses of a large tree and leave the place and wait for its decomposition to collect lastly the small bones to wear the same around neck or waist under some beliefs.

In the case of death of small child all do not go with the dead body into the forest but his/her maternal uncle or any other male member. He leaves the dead in deep forest and return back to the camp. It has also been observed that sometimes when a child is sick and about to die supposed by the Jarawa the child is left in the deep forest by a single member and thereafter the reason is said by them that he/she has gone to the Uppar chadda (Upper House in the sky).

No religion as prevailed in the society of non-Jarawas is existed among the Jarawas. Their belief, totem, myths and legends are still unknown to us outsiders. However, it is quite clear that they have some totems either, or spiritual belief which restrict the Jarawas not to kill deer and bird. It may be noted in addition that the Onges for spiritual belief do not kill the wild cat and crocodile.

In their kinship the Jarawas do not refer to their kin by using their name but by using their kinship terms. *Kaya* (mother), *wakaya* (my mother), *aamume* (father), *wamume* (my father), *mau-mame* (father's father), *mayawaya* (mother's mother), *aaikota* (younger brother/younger sister), are few of the kinship terms.

TOWARDS FRIENDSHIP

Those who do not know exactly the history of Jarawas or do not understand the tribal life and way of their defence generally called the Jarawa 'unfriendly people'. The history tells that before they came unfriendly towards the outsiders they came in contact of the outsiders with friendly gesture on several-recorded occasions. Colebrook during the first penal settlement came across some Jarawas near the present Dundas Point area and he was able to collect some Jarawa words with no skirmish. It is evident that the aborigines with whom Lieutenant Blair and others were on friendly terms included the Jarawas of the South Andamans. Furthermore, in all probabilities, those taken to Calcutta in 1790 too were Jarawas. And according to Portman many of the kitchen-middens (near and surrounding the present Port Blair) that he saw were in the areas where the Jarawa had lived, because what they contained – as pointed out to him by the rest of the Andamanese—were remains of the sort of things which only the Jarawas eat, things the other Andamanese would not even touch.

Due to some unknown reasons the Andamanese (as we know them now) had become far stronger by the time of the second occupation, and had occupied almost the entire land around the harbour, having driven the Jarawas into the hinterland.[26]

The Jarawa always distrusted the Great Andamanese with help of whom the Britishers made many attempts to capture the Jarawas and to establish friendship with them. But the Jarawas were always out of the handshake distance. On some occasions they were captured by the Britishers but the captives were either died of sickness or became so sick that they had to be released in forest. The dubious purpose of the Britishers through expeditions, captures and releases could never be achieved.

There were murders of the convicts employed in the forest and of those in the service of the Forest Department, because the Jarawas did never like the felling of Forest on their motherland and such intrusion. Therefore, in 1902 Sir Richard Temple, Chief Commissioner decided to send a punitive expedition against the Jarawas. Vaux was in-charge of the expedition, and was accompanied by Rogers, the Deputy Conservator of Forest and Bonig, Assistant Harbour Master. Mr. Vaux was to lose his life in battle against the Jarawas. The punitive expedition of the Britishers gained nothing but a life of a Britisher.

Again in 1901, another punitive expedition headed by Fawcett who was in military command was conducted but failed. Such expeditions lasted from 1901 to 1902 and onwards. But significantly nothing in favour of the Britishers was gained and not a single Jarawa was captured.

D.L. Morgan was the leader of one of the punitive expeditions. His party consisted of 12 Great Andamanese, 16 Policemen and 35 convicts had an encounter with the Jarawas on 26th Feb, 1918. But the expedition went fruitless. One more expedition was conducted by C.G. Fields accompanied by Baines, 15 policemen, 6 Great Andamanese and 40 convicts on 8th March 1921. This expedition also had proved failure.

Thus the Britishers' all efforts to befriend the Jarawa and/or to achive other dubious purposes were made failed by the patriot Jarawa. They were untamed purely.

The Jarawas till few decades back were keeping themselves far away from the outsiders entirely. One band of the Jarawa shown some signs of friendliness in 1968, the credit for which must be given to Shri Bakhtawar Singh, the then Superintendent of Police, who headed the Bush Police. It all started with three Jarawa boys who entered Kadamtala of Middle Andaman. They were captured by the Bush Police and brought to Port Blair. They were kept for a month and sent back with gifts. Thereafter, gift dropping in the area where they presumably lived was intensified. Since then the gift dropping missions began to be continued for the next few decades.

In most of the mission T. N. Pandit an anthropologist of the Antoropological Survey of India was one of the leading members. T.N. Pandit writes:

> " On 18th February 1947, a gift dropping party led by a head constable reported seeing a large group of Jarawas in FoulBay area. The Jarawa members seemed to make friendly gestures and had dropped their bows and arrows on the ground. They seemed to desire more gifts. One of them even jumped into the water and swam across to the police party in their dinghy, stayed in the dinghy for a while and then swam back to his group". Thus it became a historical event with reference to the friendly contact of Jarawa with outsiders. The gift dropping thereafter was continued under the supervision of Bakhtawar Singh on most of the occasions. The Jarawas were contacted at Yadita, FoulBay, Chotalingbang Bay and Lakralungta by the contact expedition party. But on the other hand the Jarawas of other groups were unfriendly towards the outsiders. They killed many of the settlers in different cases. It was obvious from the study that in most of the cases the neighbouring outsiders had entered the Jarawa Reserve to fish, hunt and collect the forest produces and then they were killed by the Jarawas. This is why whenever a poacher has been killed

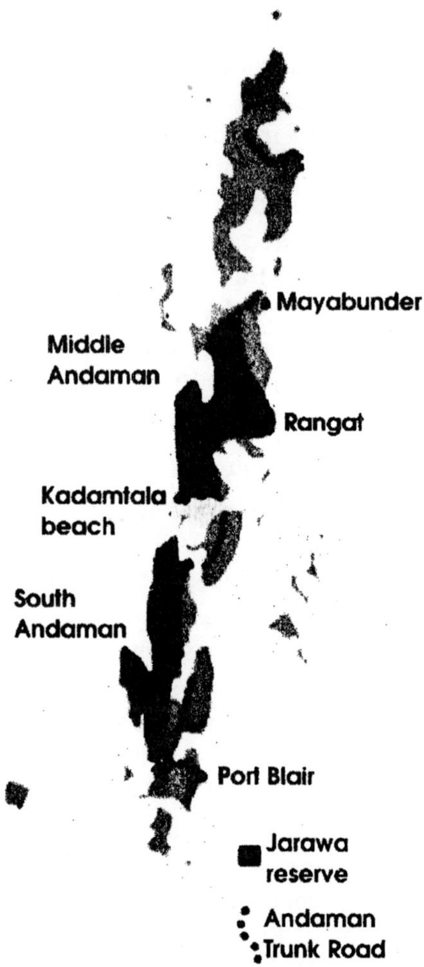

Fig. Map of Andaman and Nicobar Islands

by the Jarawas his body has been found horrifyingly mutilated. On several occasions the settlers reached the Jarawa habitat, destroyed their huts and / or took away their belongings or misbehaved with the Jarawa women in the absence of male folks and then as revenge during night hours the Jarawas entered the settlement and killed many persons. In several cases the Jarawa too entered the adjacent non-Jarawa settlements mainly at night, took away their needs like banana (they call *'chone'*), vessel (they call *'busu'*) and iron piece (they call *'taah'*) etc. and/or killed the animals.

The main settlement of outsiders where Jarawa incidents occurred were Herbertabad, Templemayo, Tirur, Collinpur, Manpur, Muslim Basti, Hobdaypur, Caddle Gunj, Tusnabad, Sonapahad, Ferrergunj, Jirkatang, Alipur, Mathura, Beachdera, Miletilak etc. in South Andaman; Adajig, Lorojig, Oralkacha, Udaygarh, settelements near Wraftess Creek in Baratang Island and Kadamtala, Phooltala, Dhaninala, Hanspuri, Chainpur, Kaushalya Nagar, Kalsi, Chainpur and Shantanu in Middle Andaman.

The Jarawas were quite unpredictable. Since the first successful contact established with the Jarawas in February, 1974 the Andaman and Nicobar Administration conducted periodical contact expedition to befriend the Jarawas and to study them which has been discontinued recently when the Jarawa themselves came into freindly contact with the outsiders.

The author has investigated among the Jarawas and the peoples in general active around the Jarawa Reserve and collected the crime cases registered with the Police in different outposts and stations. It has been revealed that out of recorded 80 cases, 49 cases of poaching under '7/8 PAT, Regulation 1956' have been recorded between 1996 and 2002 and the rest cases were of Jarawa raid/ attack mostly as revenge taken by the Jarawas. On investigation into the revenge cases it was found that in most of the cases at first the local settlers entered into their territory for hunting/fishing and collection of wood and other forest produces and/or destroyed their hut and/or looted their belongings and/or molested their women in absence of adult males. Being well acquainted with the Jarawa language the author was fortunate enough to listen such incidents occurred in past from the Jarawas themselves. Apart from the '7/8 PAT, Regulation 1956' of poaching the cases concerning the Jarawa have been registered under different Indian Penal Codes such as 147, 148, 149, 302, 307, 380, 429 and 457 etc. The Jarawas shot down several forest and APWD workers in their territory in past.

There were many APWD workers who were attacked by the Jarawas during the construction of the Andaman Trunk Road from Jirkatang to Baratang in South Andaman. Some of them are Kalimuthu and Bhimbahadur attacked on 21st April 1969 and Joseph Kujur, Emil Bara, Markose Tigga, Philmon Dungdung, Mayal Kujur, Budha Munda and Dawood Kiro attacked on 29th January 1971. Former Andaman and Nicobar Police superintendent Shri Ujwaleshwar Mishra says "the 70s saw a spurt in killings and for the first time we had cases where many PWD workers and their trucks were targeted. This coincided with the beginning of the Andaman Trunk Road ...The 80s and the 90s saw a massive increase in the attacks...189 acts of hostilities against the APWD, forest and Police personnels. This is an extremely high figure compared to the 70 acts during the 50s to the 70s. The construction of the ATR, encroachment and poaching clearly gave causes for the increase of violence on part of the Jarawas."

In the cases pertaining to murder under sections 302 and 307 IPCs the accused have been recorded as either 'Jarawa' or 'unknown' and no action could be taken against the considered accused thereof.

Their obstinate and aggressive hostility withstanding their refusal to allow any contact caused some highly specific problems to the settler population and the government for a long period.

In the same year of 'Enmay Case' (later discussed) in 1998 when the Jarawa for the first time voluntarily came into the friendly contact with the outsiders to a larger extent some important Jarawa cases were recorded.

On 2nd February 1998 the Jarawas had attacked the Police Outpost No. 4 at Tirur injuring a police constable and soon in their second attack on 5th February 1998 they attacked an old lady of Tirur. In their third attack on 10th February 1998 they killed a settler Jogin Chakraborty of Ferrargunj of South Andaman.

On 23rd April 1998 a Jarawa attack was made in the Jirkatang area when one Shri Balakrishnan R/o Jirkatang No 02 went into the Jarawa Reserve to collect *Ballies* for making fence on his land. He was shot down by the natives of the Reserve and as result he died on the spot. The case was registered under 302/34/IPC with Police Station, Bambooflat.

In an unnatural incident of its type, during the last week of January in 1998 the Jarawas attacked a group of 11 Myanmarese poachers who intruded into their territory in the west coast of Tirur village in South Andaman. Five of them were found to be dead and six were missing.

OF RECENT YEARS AND NOW

A Jarawa boy aged 14 years namely Enmay was found with his leg fractured in a nallah at Attenjig Corner in Kadamtala on 15th April 1996. He was immediately taken to G. B. Pant Hospital, Port Blair. The incident of the Jarawa boy sustaining multiple fracture was not a fall-out of any scuffle with the local population but it was simply accidental.

During the same period for the first time in the history of the Jarawa contact, four Jarawa boys were befriended near Bluff Bay in South Andaman. This occurred when the members of the contact team of the Administration on their way back after contacting the Jarawas at Lakra Lungta in Middle Andaman tried to contact the Jarawas in South Andaman and found these four Jarawa boys waving at them from the shore near Bluff Bay.

Two of the Jarawa boys swam towards the boat of the contact team and gleefully accepted the gifts. Hitherto the Jarawa of only Middle Andaman were being contacted and this was for the first time that the Jarawa of South Andaman could be brought into contact.

Over here Mr. Enmay was convalescing at the G.B. Pant Hospital, Port Blair for about six months. A sullen expression mingled with joy of being re-united with his family members were emanating from the face of Enmay when he returned to his retreat in the thickets of Middle Andaman with plenty of presents given by the Andaman & Nicobar Administration. Enmay was received by his parents alongwith 65 other Jarawas soon after the official party landed at Foul Bay at the Western coast of Middle Andaman on October, 4. Contrary to the obscure belief, the young Jarawa received a warm welcome on his arrival by his fellow beings and his parents were seen moved to happy tears at the home coming of their son. The father took him in his lap and sat quietly for hours in their traditional way of welcoming.

For the first instance of its sort in the history of Andamans, the Negrito primitive tribe Jarawa came out of their native forest habitats in the open amidst the so-called civilized population. This incident happened on October 21, 1997 when 8 Jarawas (four of them were females) came out of their habitat of Lakralungta. Again on October, 22 two Jarawas came out. In such cases they were provided with the gift items on administrative behalf. Again in morning, the residents of the area were taken by surprise when they saw as many as 63 Jarawas appeared at the Uttara Jetty. The police personnel after providing food in adequate quantity to them dropped them back to their huts (Chada) of Lakralungta. These were the first instances in the whole history of the isles when the tribes voluntarily sought to establish contact with the settlers and ventured out of the forest and into the mainstream settlements. It was particularly puzzling given the fact that Jarawas had for long been so-called hostile towards the settlers. Over the next few months there were several more reports of Jarawas coming out of their forests. Here the explanation is available for the Jarawa's curious 'coming out'. It relates to the experience of Enmay, who was injured and admitted to the G B. Pant Hospital, Port Blair for about six months. During his treatment he was looked after well with good human services and behaviour served on official behalf towards him. When Enmay recovered, he was sent back to his native habitat. Since then it is Enmay who is responsible for bringing his people out. Anthropologists explain that Enmay developed a cultural affinity to the outside world; in their view Enmay perhaps wanted others of his community to experience the outsiders' hospitality that he had received. It is this, that brought the Jarawa out of the forest. Remarkably when about 63 Jarawas appeared at Uttara Jetty, they were provided with bags of coconuts and bananas, the entire group was then brought on boats and escorted by armed policemen taken back into Jarawa territory. At the other end however more trouble was in store. Just as one of the boatmen was about to return some of the Jarawa youths seized the boatman's bamboo pole when he was pushing his boat into the creek and tried to haul him ashore. The shaken boatman said "I have interacted with the Jarawa people for many years but for the first time in my life I was afraid. I did not know what they would do to me". However some of the older women of the Jarawa who had known the boatman for long time scolded the youths and forced them to let him go. The milk of human kindness is nothing alien to the primitive Jarawa. A contact party led by Shri I.P. Gupta, Lt. Governor of Andaman and Nicobar Islands which met a large group of Jarawa men, women and children of Foul Bay in October, 1997, experienced the Jarawa kindness. The incident occurred when a cameraman accompanying the team fainted on the shore there due to the scorching sun and the sultry weather. The members of the team became utterly helpless to help the cameraman regain his lost consciousness. The Jarawas noticed him lying unconscious, some of them rushed to extend their helping hands. According to the Lt. Governor, one of the aborigines held a big leaf over the unconscious cameraman's head to protect him against the sun while another Jarawa youth massaged his body parts and thus the man was saved.

After the Jarawas have been befriended, largely their movements on ATR and towards the adjacent settlements have been increased. Working as consultant in AAJVS I was deputed on many occasions on patrolling duty in the Jarawa areas which served me full opportunity along with my duty to stay with them, study them and gain plenty of information. The Jarawas to the larger extent have come into the friendly contact with the AAJVS team. The Jarawas have their geographical movements as we observed mainly because of their kinship and for food and water. In this regard it is significant to mention that the Jarawas of Tirur area and other unknown habitats of South Andaman have come in less contact with the Jarawas of Middle Andaman and the outsiders. However, for the first time about 15-20 Jarawas came at Punnanalah area (near old dilapidated Guest House of Forest Department) during the first week of October, 2000 and constructed a hut *(Chadda)* on AndamanTrunk Road (ATR) side. Their this habitat was called '*Tullichadda*' by the Jarawas. At a distance of few kilometers ahead after B.D. Nallah another hut has been constructed on ATR side by a Jarawa family of Middle Andaman. This family was headed by Shri Chai that's why their this habitat was generally called *'Chaichadda*" by us while the Jarawa name of this habitat was *'Bimuchadda'*. Further on ATR side another hut but it is community hut, was constructed by about 40-50 Jarawas near R.K. Nallah which was located at a distance of 7 kms from Middle Strait. This was the third hut on ATR side in South Andaman. Their this hut was called '*Tuichadda*' by the Jarawas. In Middle Andaman at Dhaninallah area (25 kms. from Uttara) another hut has been constructed on ATR side by the Jarawas. They call this habitat '*Levchadda*'. '*Lev'* means honey. Because this area is highly rich in availability of honey *(lev)*, the hut here is called '*Levchadda*'. In October, 2000 there were total four huts constructed by the Jarawa on ATR side namely '*Tullichadda'*, *'Bimuchadda'*, '*Tuichadda*' of South Andaman and '*Levchadda*' of Middle Andaman.

Before the Enmay case the Jarawa never dared to make intrusion and/or raid into the adjacent revenue villages in broad day light. Reportedly from the last of 1998 onward largely the Jarawas made their intrusions into the nearby settlements with no fear for want of whatever they see of their interest being devoid of Xenophobia. Gradually they learnt the workable Hindi. In south Andaman alone more than 180 cases of Jarawa intrusion have been noticed in the last two years mostly in day time. The Tirur Jarawa entered the villages of Tusnabad, Manpur, Templemeyo, Herbertabad, Tirur, Ferrargunj, Caddlegunj, and Mathura etc. while the Jarawas of Middle Andaman appeared in the villages of Kadamtala, Phooltala, Shantanu, Kausalya Nagar, Uttara and other areas. The Jarawas of ATR usually make their raid into the Ranchi villages of Baratang area. The Jarawa members of one band accompany other in raids/attacks as observed.

On 24th Nov. 2000 during day time a large number of Jarawas of Tirur and RK Nallah made a joint raid into the south Andaman villages of Mathura, Alipur and Tusnabad in full turmoil and looted the worthy belongings of the villagers which mainly included the utensils and iron items on arrow point. They used broken Hindi and threatened the villagers. The AAJVS team headed by the author controlled the Jarawas and shifted them with help of Police truck to their native places.

On 1st March, 2002 about 150 Jarawas in many groups entered the settlements of Ferrargunj, Tirur, Caddlegunj and Manpur. They looted the belongings of one Shri Rajendran Pillai of Manpur worth around Rs. 80,000/- as sustained officially. Then the angry settlers came on agitation and stopped the traffic flow of the area for want of justice by blocking the road. Director (Tribal Welfare) and other higher officers of the local administration immediately visited the spot and promised to the angry settlers to take specific action in the matter. Thereafter the author was posted there to control the movement of the Jarawas in the area. Since then no untoward incident could take place in the area.

On Andaman Trunk Road side the Jarawa trend is highly increased to board the tops of buses and vehicles plying on ATR to move from one place to another and to contact the non-Jarawa people. As far as the Jarawa of Tirur area (South Andaman) are concerned basically their increased curiosity led them to come out of their forest.

It has been very interesting to observe that when Jarawas of one habitat killed any big prey then the Jarawas of other habitat(s) come to get share in the feast. This is another important reason of their movement from one habitat to another. Quite often it has been observed on ATR. Usually they board tops of buses/other vehicles to reach the destination (Jarawa habitat) to eat pork *('Wowe')* or to reach any location to hunt or fish or for other economic gain. The Andaman Administration has made all efforts at possible level to stop the Jarawa from boarding the vehicles.

The Jarawa have their own names for different zones / location of the islands. The Jarawa name for Baratang is '*Tanmadeda Nayami*', for Middle Strait area is *'Elentilipad'* and for Kadamtala is '*Kewkaab*'. '*Tanmad*' is the name given for Spike Island. Some Jarawa habitats with their Jarawa names are given below.

Jarawa Habitat /Location	Jarawa Name
A place in Middle Andaman	Thulugachadda
A place in South Andaman	Topochadda
A place in South Andaman	Keneakka
Lakralungta	Onnechadda
R. K. Nallah area	Tuichadda
Dhaninallah area	Levchadda
A place in Tirur (South Andaman)	Lavaitala
Potatang of South Andaman	Chukulu

There are many other Jarawa camp areas in South Andaman especially the interior parts of Tirur area, some of which are still unvisited. Some names of the Jarawa camps along the coast (as per the Jarawa call) are *Koipotale, Ulithotalo, Utalibigiji, Urugyevalui* and *Olahe.*

As far as the Jarawa movement from one island to another island is concerned, generally they swim across the creek mainly during low tide. Mainly they have two ways of migration. The first is along with Middle Andaman. They reach South Andaman from Middle Andaman or to Middle Andaman from South Andaman via Spike-2 Island and Bluff Island by swimming mainly during low tide. The Jarawas take rest or get camped temporarily on these said tiny islands. This region of Jarawa swimming has many tiny islands around the Spike-2 Island. These islands are Bingham Island, Bluff Island, Mangrove Island, Spike-2 Island, Stoat Island and Talabaicha (talakaicha) Island Sanctuaries. Further to the north in Middle Andaman, the Jarawas are living in hutments scattered in the north-west coast of Roberts' Bay situated just opposite of JPP Luis-in-Let-Bay. Jarawa in low tide after crossing the creek by swimming enter into the settlements like Hanspuri, Bojotta and Chainpur of Mayabunder. The second route of migration is between Baratang Island and South Andaman. Through this way they reach from one island to another by swimming. While passing by swimming they take refuge on Lal Tikrey called *"Vaada"* in Jarawa language which is located near Wraftess Creek between Baratang and South Andaman. In the said second route of Jarawa movement the Jarawa usually come from South Andaman to reach some non-tribal settlements of Baratang. These settlements are Naya dera, Mirchi Tikrey, 3 No. Vilar, Wraftess Creek, Khatta Khadi, Katan, Jarawa Creek and Baludera etc. There are more than 200 households in these settlements. The people of these settlements have been on several occasions annoyed by the Jarawa turmoil. On most of the occasions the Jarawas have plundered their plantation and took away the iron pieces, metal objects, vessels, cloths and other items of their need. In all cases of Jarawa looting in the adjacent settlements they never looted the cash and jewel etc. to use in the ways that are in vogue in the so-called civilized society. They entered the non-tribal villages either to take revenge or to acquire their required simple items.

Since the Jarawas are daring foragers and good swimmers, they have no difficulty in crossing the creeks and nallah. It is observed that they use simple raft to bring their belongings with them while swimming. Old ladies, children and patients to cross creek or nallah preferably use raft. However, in course of my visit to Jarawa camped locations such raft very rarely could be seen. Previously the Jarawas used canoe but whether they made canoe themselves or collected, is yet not clearly known. The art of making canoe is unknown to the present Jarawa as observed.

As a frequent contact with the non-autochthons the Jarawa community underwent rapid changes. The predominant diseases and conditions were identified to be measles, pneumonia, acute upper and lower Respiratory Tract Infection and fungal infections on skin from time to time. The Jarawas have voluntarily accepted the modern mode of treatment for which they are voluntarily coming out of their forest to different contact points to be treated/ evacuated. The Jarawa Tourism on the ATR (Andaman Trunk Road) has been a burning problem of these days. Increased visits are made by the tourists by private vehicles on ATR just to have a glance of the Jarawas. In such visits they try to contact the Jarawa by way of giving gifts and taking photographs with them. The population of the area adjacent to the Jarawa territory is increasing day by day with the increase in their activities which are adversely affecting the Jarawa life. The young Jarawa members began to stop the travelers on the ATR for taking snacks and other gifts and for transportation. To attract the travelers the Jarawa children somersault on the ATR. In doing so many of the Jarawa community have met road accidents as result of which they were injured and to lose their parts. For example: Tauthe (M 12) got his hand fractured and bent, Gillet (M 10) lost his left hand, Othahene (M 06) got his right leg bent and Anthawa (M 15) got his left leg bent, etc. With the end of their hostility towards the outsiders and establishment of their friendship with the others the Jarawas are vulnerable to new and alien diseases against which they have no indigenous immunity.

The Jarawa physiology is quite unique in some respects; having different health parameters of blood pressure, body temperature etc. compared to non-Jarawas. Their fatty food intake is comparatively high but they do not suffer coronary and heart diseases obviously because of their unique fat metabolism. Now they underwent the dietary change with change of taste. Non-salty tongue has become salty tongue. They are now in addiction of tobacco introduced by the non-Jarawas. The habit of chewing tobacco and pan among the Jarawas is recently introduced mostly by the policemen, forest and APWD workers, shopkeepers and general public. As another noteworthy result of the contact between the Jarawa and the non-Jarawa they have started to keep the dogs with them. Unwashed cloth has recently arrived in the material culture of the Jarawa.

THE SHOMPENS

Shompens are the only mongoloid primitive tribes of these islands. As per the author's enumeration they are 250-300 in number (approx.) today and inhabited in different terrain in Great Nicobar. They are semi-nomadic people shifting their camps from one location to another depending on the availability of food and water. They are mainly located at 24 km (Diggu Camp), 27 km (Kothangai Camp), 35 km, 37 km on East West Road, Alexandria river area, Galathia river area (Jantam), Kopenheat, Pilokunji, Kokeon (Ionie), Inhenglo, Pilobha, Pilobet, Laful, Trinket and Jhaonallah (Ranganathan Bay) etc. The Great Nicobar Island is the southern most island of Andaman and Nicobar Groups of India situated between 6^0 45' and 7^0 15' North latitudes and 93^0 37' and 93^0 56' East longitudes. The Nicobarese of this island call the Shompens "Shamhap". It is a Nicobari term meaning "those who live in the forest". Some Nicobarese and other settlers call them "Champion". The Shompens do not identify themselves as "Shompen". The west coast Shompen call themselves *'Kalay'*, whereas the east coast Shompen call themselves '*Keyet*'. One Shompen band call people of other Shompen band '*Buaeia'*.

The inland tribe is split into two main divisions viz. those who inhabit the interior parts of dense forest and those who form camps near to the coast. The Shompens of coastal area are generally called *'Mawas'* who are in frequent contact with the Nicobarese and fishermen.

They are short statured with yellow and yellow-brown skin and wavy hair.

Man (1886: 173) observed:

> This island tribe, only a ramnant of which now remains is more or less confined to the interior region of the one island of Great Nicobar (the largest island of the southern group). He considered this tribe to be the aborginial stock of the Nicobarese. Their singular purity of breed, even at the present time seems to point to this, for other sections and coast tribes even in Great Nicobar show traces of admixture with Malay and other stocks.
>
> The inference I have ventured to draw from all the informations and facts that have come to my knowledge is that the presence in modern times of the Shompen in one island only of the group is due to the determination of those who showed themselves hostile to them in other islands, so they became fugitives, finding refuge where they could be sure to live without fear of molestation.

The unmixed origin of the Shompens appears to be indicated by the singular unfirmity of type observable even among sections of the tribe so widely separated as to be ignorant of each other's existence.[27]

Man says that the Shompens were the original inhabitants of Great Nicobar and that a later date they were driven into the interior by aliens more powerful than themselves who were wrecked on their coast.

Sir R. Temple (1901) contradicts this saying:

> There is no racial difference between a Shompen and other Nicobarese. The difference are merely such as exist between islands and as are to be expected among people living an almost isolated existence. Kloss believed that the Shompens were an isolated group of primitive Malayans.
>
> In terms of the blood groups the Shompen present a picture so far unknown in any of the primitive tribes of South-east

Asia. All the 55 Shompens tested belong to the 'O' group. The complete absence of *p* and *q* genes in the Shompen population who had migrated to this island in a small group can be explained if we presume that the ancestors had a very high frequency of 'O' genes. The sickle cell trait is almost entirely absent in the Shompen population.[28]

The existence of the Shompen was first mentioned by Pastor Rosen, a Danish missionary in 1831. In 1846 Admiral Steen Bille paid the first recorded visit when the islands were annexed by the British Government. De-Roepstorff paid three visits and found a temporary encampment of Shompen. E.H. Man made contact with the Shompen in 1884 and his finding served first hand informations on many Shompen issues to the outsiders. The findings of Boden Kloss and Anderson have also been of great significance.

The general pattern of housing among the Shompens is adopted to the physical character of the ground. They build their houses as near as possible to the source of fresh drinking water. The Shompens of east coast remain close to the sea-shore or in the valleys while the west coast Shompens prefer the interior and the slopes of hills. During a visit to the interior forest I observed that the Shompens of interior parts generally do not display the approach roads to their actual camps and simply don't clear the way to their hut for they do not want any alien person to visit their camps.

The settlement pattern of the Shompens is of the fragmented type. They build their huts on raised platform with support of piles at height of 1-3 meters from the surface. The hut is carefully constructed with the roof of palm leaves. They use bamboo, cane and fibre in making walls of hut. Sometimes they build their hut adjacent to a tree for the strong support. Houses are mostly rectangular in shape but can also be seen in the square shape. Sometimes they build temporary hut at a place where alongwith fishing or hunting or both, they take rest.

List of some Major Items in Shompen Indigenous Diet

1. Pandanus (Kewri / Munkung)*(Pandanus tectoria)*
2. Komba (*Pynanga coastata*)
3. Wild boar (*Sus-scorpa*)
4. Long tailed, black faced monkey *(Presbytes entellus achates)*
5. Python (*Python Reticulatus)*
6. Monkey (*Crab eating macaque*)
7. Water monitor (*Varanus salvator*)
8. Crocodile of salt water *(Crocodilus palustris)*
9. Turtle (*Erectmochelys* Sp.)
10. Turtle egg.
11. Megapode bird *(Megapode Freycinet nicobarensis)*
12. Egg of Megapode bird.
13. Snake (for adult only).
14. Crab
15. Wood insects and other insects.
16. Varieties of fish
17. Nicobari pigeon (*Caloneas nicobarica)*
18. Pied imperial pigeon (*Dueula bicolour)*
19. Cater pillar
20. Mussel
21. Lobster
22. Wild pig (*Sus- nicobarensis)*
23. Tuber of Dioscoria plant
24. Colocasia (*Rhyzomes)*
25. Tacca (*Rhyzomes)*
26. Wild coconut
27. Wild banana

28. Wild mango (*Mangifera andamanica)*
29. Papaya
30. Wild Arecanut(*Areca triandra)*
31. Wild betel leaf
32. Lemon
33. Chillie
34. Honey and
35. Others.

The flesh of frog is also consumed by the Shompens. Interestingly the flesh of monkey is mainly consumed by the Shompens of interior forest. Komba stem is eaten raw. The Shompens drink cane water during the days of water scarcity. Pandanus, crab, fish and reptiles are simply boiled or roasted. The use of lemon, chillies, papaya and tobacco etc. has evidently been acquired from the outsiders. Shompens of coastal areas have started to prepare and consume rice-dal, as a result of their outside contact. They keep dogs and small piggeries. The Shompens do not know the art of preparation of any alcoholic beverage but often collect toddy (Coconut beer) from the neighbouring Nicobarese. To have an approach to the raised platform of the hut a crude type of ladder is made out of pole or bamboo. The smallness of the huts are perhaps due to the hilly ground, tropical climate and temporary nature of stay in a particular locality. The Shompen huts are of primitive type and differ from those found in the rest of Nicobars. Mainly their houses are built of wood, cane and leaves. Sometimes they build hut of no walls but with thatched roof. The doors and windows can also be seen in a Shompen hut called '*Kachaam*' in their language. The door is called '*Kanau*' in the Shompen language while '*Aegania*' is said for the ladder. The roof of hut is called '*Tawaef*'.

The Shompens construct piggery beneath their hut. In one of my visits at Shompen habitats, underneath the platform of a hut which was located near Galathea river I was surprised to see that they grew tobacco plants in plenty. They are madly fond of tobacco.

Over the space separated for the kitchen a thick layer of earth or a piece of tin is always placed to protect the hut from the hazard of fire. A rope can also be seen hanging towards the earth from the door of the raised hut, which is generally used by the females and old members to get down.

The Shompens wear indigenous cloth called *'loe'* in their language which is prepared from bark sheets of trees (*Ficus and Sterculia macrophylla*). But they almost entirely gave up the wearing of bark cloth which now has been substituted by the textile. The women started wearing '*lungi*' after it has been introduced to them by the outside world. With *'lungi'* they go topnaked quite often but sometimes blouse can be seen on them. The men wear '*langoti*' only. The Shompens of Dagmar, Galathia, Trinket and east coast area wear second hand shirts with *'langoti'* while women second hand blouses. Some males began to wear both lungi and banyan at a time. These second hand garments they receive from the fishermen from Campbell Bay or other neighbouring non-Shompens in illegal barter system. Some cases of such exchange have been noticed in which the Shompens gave them their canoe, honey and Rudraksha of their collection and received second hand loin or cotton cloths, implements and vessels etc. under the illegal barter. The Shompens do not use any foot wear. Both the sexes adorn themselves with bead necklaces, bangles and bind strip of spathe or piece of cloth round the head. Their earlobes are pierced almost commonly to enable them to wear long strips of bamboos or canes called '*ahav*' in Shompen language. They are very fond of the necklaces made of Oysters and grains of grass. During his visit the author noticed every one demanded '*mala*' (garland made of plastic pearl, fibre etc.). They wear another type of garland also which is made of Rudraksha (*Eliocarpus gangestus*). Their conical earplug is made of cane or soft wood with front pointed.

A Shompen family is generally consisted of husband-wife and their unmarried children. After marriage a couple construct a new hut and live separately. When a Shompen marries more than one woman then both the wives and their children share the same hut and hearth. Shri Mingi, Shompen of Trinket bay after the death of his brother kept his wife with him alongwith his own one. The practice of polygyny is quite often in vogue among the Shompens. The family size varies between one and ten persons.

As far as status of women in Shompen community is concerned they are believed to be most sensitive members, the safety of whom is the prime concern for the Shompens. They do not allow any outsiders generally to see their adult female members with the fear of their possible abduction. The women are not allowed to move freely outside their camp premises without the permission of the head of family.

There are many divisions and bands among the Shompens but how and on which basis the divisions have been formed, yet not known to us. It is observed that some bands deliberately live having no link with some certain bands for the reason unknown. It is probable that band interaction is existed among them.

The economic system of the Shompens is technologically primitive. The Shompens are mainly herders and horticulturists. Besides gardening, they engage themselves in hunting, fishing, gathering and the domestication of pigs. Apart from it their basket making, manufacturing of accessories related to economic activities and barter are still continued.

There were three kinds of economy among the Shompens viz. Subsistence economy, Barter economy and Gift economy categorized on the basis of activities, particularly the amount of labour and time put therein, on an average day. The subsistence economy is predominant activity, barter economy is subordinate activity and gift economy had no activity on the part of Shompen. Now providing of gift items by the AAJVS to the Shompens has been stopped completely under a firmed policy. But the gift economy particularly still exists in their contact with the neighbouring settlers. All efforts are made by the local Administration to stop such illegal contact. The subsistence economy and the Barter economy have the close relationship with each other. The commodities the Shompens get through their subsistence economic activities became a part of Barter economy. These commodities are bartered by the Shompens with the Nicobarese while some commodities are bartered with the administrative representatives and in this system the representatives give them their required items like rice, pulse, cloth and implement etc. Under the subsistence economy aboriculture, hunting, fishing, gathering, apiculture and domestication of animals are included. Aboriculture is one of the major occupations of Shompens. They raise colocasia, lemon, green chilli, banana, tobacco, betel, betelnut, tapoica and coconut around their huts.

Before the advent of dog, the hunting of pig was mere strenuous and less certain as the Shompens had to chase the pig themselves to spear it. The dogs now have become of great relevance for the Shompens in their hunting. They generally fish in river, shallow water and the creeks with the help of indigenous spear. Their outrigger canoe is used in navigation and fishing.

Apiculture of the Shompens is very simple. When bees accommodate in a hollow of tree trunk which is made by the Shompen, the hollow is regularly watched by the tribal members. When a matured hive is built the Shompen harvest the honey. They use the juice of pinanga leaves in driving away the bees from the body. This juice is smeared on the body before going in for honey collection.

The game of hunting, fishing and gathering are major activities in their subsistence economy. While moving in the forest along the shore line miscellaneous objects are found by them, if they think those of their use further in any respect they bring them to their camp; such items are halves of drum, buoy, plastic bottle and cane etc. There is a high demand of items like Rudraksha (*Eliocarpus gangestus*) and buoy, etc. in the local market.

The Shompens do not kill the piglings but adult pigs and sows. Apart from the simple direct barter the Shompens have another barter system 'Indirect Barter'. Under this system the tribes place the commodities at a certain spot and return back and after few days or hours they come there and find some commodities of their requirement such as machetes, cloth, tobacco, bundle of beedis, daos and other items while in the process the tribes keep honey, lemon, resin, buoy, rudraksha etc. on the spot. This system is practiced by the neighbouring Nicobarese with the Shompen since long period.

Shompens do not know the art of making bow and arrow. They generally use spear which is made with bamboo/wood and cane for the purpose of hunting and fishing. They make spear with iron also which is called *'hanoom'* in their language. Their plucker is made of iron and bamboo/wood to pluck the pandanus and fruits. Matchete is made of iron for miscellaneous purposes. It is very interesting to see their Fire-generator made of dry wood of Inbot-plant to produce fire. Their piggling is made of wood/ cane and bamboo is used to house the pigglings. They use cane basket to store the materials while bark box is used for the same purpose. They use Brochette of iron rod /bamboo to boil fish. Their Gouge of bamboo / wood and iron is used in collection of larvae. Their bamboo made Oar or Rudder is used to direct the canoe. Their outrigger canoe is made of wood for navigation, fishing and miscellaneous purpose.

For making outrigger canoe the Shompen use following wood species - *Amoora Wallinchi king, Barringtonia asiatica* (L) Kurtz, *Autocarpus chapleosha rexb, Calaphyllum Sonlattri burm* etc. Their dao of iron is of immense importance among to the Shompens. Chisel, hammer and axe are the other articles they use.

The Shompens produce fire by a primitive method. A dry wood of Inbot plant *(Stercullia alata)* is divided into two parts. One part is chiselled into a cylindrical rod with round pointed end and the other part is flattened with a small groove on it. The pointed end of the first part is placed on the small groove of the second part. Then some dry straw pieces or burnable dust are kept near the edges of groove and then fast churn is given on the groove by the first part which produces heat. The heat captures the dust or soft small pieces of dry straw and as result with the burning of straw / dust the fire is produced.

The Shompen has no special ritual related to pregnancy. However, there are some restrictions on the pregnant woman during her later stage of pregnancy. A separate hut is constructed for the delivery of the child. At the time of delivery old women are the special attendants to look after the mother and new born child. On the second day of birth, lime paste is applied on forehead of the child and of the mother as well. A mark or cross is made on the baby's stomach to protect him/her from the evil spirits. Open fire is placed near to the sleeping mother and baby. The first semisolid food for the baby includes pandanus paste and honey mainly.

Abduction, exchange and negotiation are the ways of choosing life partner among the Shompens. Along with monogamy, polygyny is also practiced. One can easily observe the huge disparity between the age of husband and that of his wife. They don't have any special ceremony pertaining to marriage.

The incidents of marriage between Shompen and non- Shompen have also been noticed. During my visit to Shompen camps in 1998 many such ways of marriage I noted in my diary. Mug a Shompen girl who was adopted by Shri Sitaram, head of Chingen village married a Ranchi labourer who used to come to the village frequently. But soon after his marriage he left her alone and ran away. Then a Shompen youth namely Girth became second husband of Mug. In another case a Shompen girl got married with a coastal Nicobari boy. This girl too had been adopted by Shri Sitaram. In one case of Ranganathan Bay a widow got married with her nephew. Among the Shompens there are the following ways of acquiring lifepartner - widow marriage, widower marriage, polygyny, levirate, sororate, monogamy, and other unknown.

A dead is buried among the Shompens. When a person dies, the dead body is immediately brought out of the hut and placed on the ground in open. Then the body after the wooden bier is prepared, is tied to it with cane or fibre. Remarkably the hands are kept open not tied. A small group goes into the deep forest to hunt a pig. Meanwhile the path bearers bring the bier out of the village / camp. Before burying the corpse a hunted pig is sacrificed. The corpse is then untied and placed inside the grave on Komba leaves. Again Komba leaves in large quantity are thrown into the grave. All the materials especially the implements belonging to the dead person are kept inside the grave along with the corpse and then the grave is closed. On the next day the Shompen leave the place where the death occurred.

The Shompens believe in the existence of malevolent and benevolent spirits. The supposition generally is, that a supernatural power causes and controls all those phenomenon. They believe that Moon is the Supreme Goddess responsible for creation of earth, heaven and universe as a whole, so the Moon is their Godmother. She created a primaeval couple – husband and wife, a mythical pair of giant pigs – a sow and a boar, Satans with their nymphets and primogenitor Shompens themselves. They believe that a death after a prolonged illness is the curse of Satan while a sudden death is caused by the Goddess Moon. The Shompens see their primogenitors residing with the Goddess in the form of scars on Moon. As per the Shompen belief, the Goddess has no husband but all the creatures including Shompens are her issues. They propitiate the spirits while preparing food, going to forest for hunting and while going out to sea to fish. The members at work in the canoe and while bringing out the canoe to the sea for the first time propitiate the spirit(s).

The social organization of the Shompens is based on tradition, kinship and locality. In a family the eldest male member becomes the head who keeps control over all the family affairs.

The Shompens have a trade relations with the Nicobarese for a long time. It has been observed that behind the friendly relationship sometimes the Shompens are exploited material istically in different ways by the neighbouring Nicobarese. Exchange of commodities is the base of such relationship. Influence of the Nicobarese is clearly visible among the Shompens of Galathea region. The head of the Chingen village (a Nicobari village) accommodated a Shompen family headed by Kagaz in a separate house in his village. The Shompen family members have adapted themselves to the traditional Nicobari life style.

Two orphan children namely Koken and Abo were brought to Chingen village after their parents died of food poisoning at Pilokunji area. They are now being taken care by Shri Sitaram

THE SENTINELESE

The negrito Sentinelese live in North Sentinel Island, 64 km south west of Port Blair. The Onges call them 'Chanku ate'. They are perhaps one of the most isolated tribal communities of the present world geographically and socially. Shooting with bow-arrow against any outsider trying to land on their abode island is their traditional way to ensure their safe and undisturbed life. The north Sentinel Island is not only defended by its belligerents but also by the rough and turbulent sea supported by an unbroken ring of treacherous coral reefs. Thus it is purely dangerous except for few calm months to approach.

Many past attempts by all sorts of people ranging from administrative officials, politicians, naval officers and anthropologists to policemen to land on the North Sentinel Island have been failed in gaining the goal.

In 1880 an expedition under M.V. Portman successfully accomplished the first known landing on the North Sentinel Island. They stayed for a fortnight. During their stay the Sentinelese disappeared from the area. A woman and four children were nevertheless captured and kept for few days in the ship. Later they were released with gifts. The help of the Onges and the Aka-bea tribes were also obtained to establish friendly relationship with the Sentinelese but the scientists finally had to be frustrated and give up the idea. M.V. Portman visited the island on 15th February, 1895 with some Onges from the north Quince Island.

The second recorded landing was made on 27th August 1883. On 26th August, 1883 a gun fire was heard at irregular intervals from a distance and it was thought to be signal from a ship in trouble. On the next day Mr. Portman went to search out the unknown vessel around Rutland Island, Labyrinth group and the North Sentinel Island. He landed on the North Sentinel Island and found some deserted villages of the natives. They left some gifts for them and when they returned back to Port Blair it became clear that the heard gunfire was the volcanic cataclysm of Mt. Krakatoa explored near Java.

The first official census after independence in 1949 and 1951 failed to record the Sentinelese.

The unrecorded occasional poachings and landing of ship wrecked sailors increased the sense of xenophobia (fear of outsiders) among the Sentinelese. As late as March 1970, a wreck was spotted on a coral bed off the south east coast. On inspection it was found to have been living there for last few months. No sign of the crew was found. Atleast one escaped Indian convict from Port Blair is known to have made his way to North Sentinel Island in 1896. But the convict was killed by the Sentinelese and his body was found by a British party on the beach.

Two international ships viz. M.V. Primrose and M.V. Rusley have wrecked by a grounding on the coral reefs in the shallow water of the North Sentinel Island recently. A major chunk is still left on the spot. These two ships have been auctioned away to the crap dealers.

Now what is the official policy towards the Sentinelese succinctly mentioned below:

> "The island is totally isolated and is not open to any sort of colonization. It is the firm policy of the local administration not to interfere in life of the Sentinelese. The administration however keeps a vigil to prevent the possible intrusion by any poacher into the waters around the North Sentinel Island. This is in order to prevent the exploitation of the natural resources on the island and its territorial waters by the non-tribals and also to prevent physical contact with Sentinelese to avoid possible introduction of alien diseases to which the natives have no immunity."

Unfortunately notwithstanding the official policies and statements, repeated gift giving visits through expeditions to befriend the Sentinelese following the way of Britishers to some extent have been organized by the local administration. But with the passage of time the authority has well understood the matter and minimized their contact expeditions.

After a long gap of two years to assess the factual situation an expedition was organized by the administration in April 2003. A contact expedition led by the then Chief Secretary of Andaman and Nicobar Administration accompanied by the Secretary (Tribal Welfare), Director (Tribal Welfare), other administrative officers and the author has been conducted. In the morning of 15/04/2003 the contact party came out of the mother boat in two small out boats and reached the shallow water of the North Sentinel Island. On seeing us with coconuts there were 40-50 natives who were hidden and watching us came out on the sandy beach from the nearby bushes. Some adult male members began to ply their canoes with help of long poles instead of oar and they soon reached at a close distance of few meters from us. It was very dangerous situation for us as we by then came within the domain of their arrow range. To avoid any untoward incident and the physical contact we forthwith dropped the dehusked coconuts (a dehusked coconut is floatable) into the sea for them and returned back to the mother boat safely.

There is no doubt that the Sentinelese are still the undisputed lords of their island living in complete isolation from the outside world.

4

The Welfare Activities for the Primitive Tribes

Prior to Independence the British and Japanese policy of isolation left the tribals to themselves and almost no efforts were made to develop them except some efforts to contact and befriend them mainly for peaceful colonization and administration.

Elwin (1939) supported the establishment of sort of 'National Park' of the tribals and advised that their contact with outside world should be reduced to the minimum. Again in 1941 he supported the idea of 'isolationism' to a great extent.

During the initial period of occupation, the British cleared some 140 acres of land for cultivation, which rose to 355 acres with an additional 724 acres of land being later deforested. Subsequently about 3000 acres of land were cleared and 876 acres were brought under cultivation. This led the tribes to go back far away from the colonies, leaving the territory, which they considered of their own. In 1870, during the rule of Lord Mayo, many convicts were given freedom of movement and were encouraged to marry convict women with the idea of settling them and expanding agriculture in the islands. With increase in the number of convict population, requirement of food naturally rose and the local production of vegetables and other food items needed an immediate expansion. Under these circumstances agriculture was encouraged in the islands in south of Port Blair. By the end of the year 1894-95, 22.306 acres of land were cleared and 10.40 acres of land were cultivated of which the Government plantation of tea, coffee, cocoa, coconut and vegetables occupied 4.425 acres and the remaining land was cultivated by convict settlements.

In 1883, the Forest Department was established. The exploitation of timber from the forest was already taking place since the formation of penal colony in these islands.

The plight of the tribal communities was further aggravated by the enunciation and implementation of the National Forest Policy in 1894 by the British, which curbed the traditional rights of the tribals in forest.

Efforts were also made to take the aboriginals to the mainland and other parts. But the efforts went in vain in obtaining the consent of the responsible persons like Mauvat, Haughton, Corbyn, Homfray, Man and Portman. Against this tribal scenario after India gained Independence, in the Andaman and Nicobar Islands the Government has undertaken certain preventive, protective and progressive measures for the welfare of the Primitive Tribes. Accordingly, a firmed policy towards tribal welfare has been evolved. Pt. Jawaharlal Nehru, the first Prime Minister of Free India suggested that the approach should be to develop the 'synthesis' or 'integration' without destroying the rare and precious values of tribal people.

Pt. Jawaharlal Nehru laid down five fundamental principles, which are known as '**Tribal Panchsheel**':

1. People should develop alongwith the time of their own genius and we should avoid imposing anything on them. We should try to encourage in everything their own traditional art and culture.
2. Tribal rights in land and forest should be respected.
3. We should try to train and build up a team of their people to do the work of administration and development. Some

technical personnel from outside will no doubt be needed, especially in the beginning. But we should avoid introducing too many outsiders into tribal territory.

4. We should not over administer these areas or overwhelm them with a multiplicity of schemes, we should rather work through and not in rivalry to, their own social and cultural institutions.
5. We should judge results not by statistics or the amount of money spent, but the quality or human character that is evolved.

Presently all the welfare activities are alongwith the Nehruvian policy, the friendly policy towards the tribals.

Under the Andaman & Nicobar Islands (Protection of Aboriginal Tribes) Regulation, 1956 no non-tribal can enter the tribal areas without the permission of the competent authority. No one can exploit the resources, conduct trade and business or acquire tribal property without the permission of the Administrator. The poachers and the exploiters are booked and punished under this law. In addition substantial areas in the islands are demarcated 'Tribal Reserve' under Andaman & Nicobar Islands (Protection of Aboriginal Tribes) Regulation, 1956. The following are the designated tribal reserves.

1. 11,900 ha. on Great Nicobar Island, for the Shompens.
2. 25,200 ha. on Little Andaman Island, for the Onges.
3. 6,00 ha. on North Sentinel Island, for the Sentinelese.
4. 60 ha. on Strait Island, for the Great Andamanese.
5. 63,886 ha. on the western part of Middle & South Andaman Islands, for the Jarawas.

For the welfare of the Jarawas western parts of South Andaman and Middle Andaman have been declared 'Jarawa Reserve' which starts from the mouth of Constance Bay proceeds to Yeratil Jig including Needhan beach, Bluff and Spike Island mainly and then proceeds via Wolaga Boilu, Melagar Boilu and Mor Boilu Creeks upto the Bush Police camp No. 32 facing the luice Inlet Bay. On its eastern side the 'Jarawa Reserve' has been given an imaginary boundary alongwith the Andaman Trunk Road. The Jarawa Reserve includes coastal water upto the distance of 3 kms from the shoreline. The said declaration was made on 19th July 1979 and officially it has been decided to review the 'Jarawa Reserve' and if necessary the amendment be made in near future.

After its formation on 25th March 1976, Andaman Adim Janjati Vikas Samiti (AAJVS) is working with the main objectives i.e. to prevent extinction of the tribes, protect them, promote the socio-economic development of the tribes, solve the tribal problems and to develop the socio-economic environment essential to the survival and growth of the tribes. The Andaman Adim Janjati Vikas Samiti (AAJVS) is a society registered under the Societies Registration Act 1860 and it came into existence remarkably during 1976. The Samiti was set up on the recommendation of the Advisory Committee on Primitive Tribal Groups in Andaman & Nicobar Islands. The Hon'ble Lieutenant Governor, A & N Islands is the Chairperson of AAJVS.

The AAJVS is funded by the Central Government through Special Central Assistance (SCA) and Grant-in-aid by A & N Administration to carry out the policies and programme of the administration for well being of the Primitive Tribes.

Shompens are the Mongoloid Primitive Tribes inhabiting different parts of the Great Nicobar Island. To extend the health care to Shompen and to coordinate the welfare activities for them, one Shompen Hut Complex (SHC) in the year 1984 has been constructed at a distance of 27 km on East West Road from Campbell Bay. It was 'inaugurated on 08th May 1984. In the premises of Shompen Hut Complex the facilities of Ashram School, Medical Sub-Centre, supply of electricity and water have been provided. One Trekking Assistant with a Research Investigator (author) have been appointed in the field to implement the welfare programme at ground level and look after the Shompen aspects. The Shompens usually come to the Complex and they bring arecanut, resin, honey, lemon and Rudraksh. But after a huge landslide in the August 2002 on Eastwest road the SHC has become inaccessible through vehicle for the functionaries. The author visited the SHC from Campbell Bay on 10th Dec. 2003 by a marathon walk of about eight hours and he found that in addition to the landslide that has damaged the road at different places the Nature-mother has laid down her green carpet of grass and bushes on the road. As result the contact between the outsiders including the official functionaries and the Shompens has marginally been reduced. Since the Shompens have no clear perception about the cash money, the AAJVS under Exchange System collect the Minor Forest Produces (MFPs) and model canoe, etc. brought by the Shompens and sell these items in the open market at Campbell Bay and deposit the sale amount in the bank in common account for Shompens. The Assistant Commissioner, Campbell Bay send the receipt of the sold MFPs to the office of the AAJVS and this office in turn deposit the equal amount in the bank in common account for Shompen. This account is operated by the Assistant Commissioner, Campbell Bay who has been designated as Officer-in-charge, Shompen Hut Complex. Whenever the Shompens come to Campbell Bay and demand for iron implements, clothes, food items or any other items of requirement, these items are being supplied to them from the fund available in the common account. The coconut plantations were raised at Lawful, Kopenheat, Trinket Bay and Chingen village for the Shompens. A small plantation cum-orchard has been raised within the Shompen Hut Complex premises.

Out station rural area Gramin Telephone has been provided with Shompen Hut Complex to establish a firmed communicational link between the Shompen Hut Complex and responsible authorities.

Recently after a visit of Shri Som Naidu, Executive Secretary, AAJVS to the Great Nicobar Island in October 2000, it has been decided that rice in adequate quantity to be distributed among the Shompen from three distributing points at least, under Below Poverty Line (BPL) provision.

The Onges are pure Negrito tribes now settled at two places viz. Dugong Creek and South Bay in Little Andaman Island. The Onge Settlement at Dugong Creek was set up 1976-77 while the Onges of South Bay came into being around 1980. After the establishment of Dugong Creek settlement the Onges of Jackson Creek were rehabilitated at Dugong Creek. There were 26 and 6 wooden houses constructed for the Onges of Dugong Creek and South Bay respectively. The houses with raised platforms have been allotted among the heads of the Onge families. The Andaman Public Work Department (APWD) has undertaken the repair work of Onge houses and other old buildings and out of 26 huts, 15 huts were repaired.

A 24 kW Diesel Generator set has been established at Dugong Creek (1979) and a 15 kW electric generator set has also been installed at South Bay. A solar Power plant was established at Dugong Creek for the Onges on 23rd January 1993. Streetlights were provided to the settlements with approach footpath. A primary school has been functioning since 1978. Previously the classes were conducted in the community hall but now a separate building has been constructed for the above purpose. The Central Institute of Indian Languages (CIIL), Mysore has prepared primers for school going children on Onge-Hindi-English languages in 1994-95.

A Co-operative Society namely '*Onge Multipurpose Co-operative Society (OMPCS)*' has been formed in 1977 with the aim to collect coconuts, resin, honey, cane etc. from the Onge and to sell and give benefit to Onges. Cash economy was introduced among the Onge by raising coconut plantation. Presently 45 acres of land is covered with the coconut plantation at Dugong Creek and 10 acres at South Bay. The Onges are collecting the nuts and sell it to the OMPCS (Onge Multipurpose Co-operative Society) Dugong Creek. The OMPCS sells the nuts to the Marketing Federation at a prescribed rate. From sell proceeds from the nut a partial amount is deposited in the common account of the Onge accorded to the total nuts collected by the Onges in a month and balance is deposited in the OMPCS. All the Onges are members of the society and the chief of the Onges is the President of the society. The account of the Onge is jointly operated by the Tehsildar, Little Andaman, who has been designated as secretary of the society and Social Worker of the Dugong Creek Settlement as treasurer.

One Medical Officer-in-charge is posted in Dugong Creek who takes health care of the Onges of Dugong Creek and South Bay. The Medical Officer is assisted by the ANM, Pharmacist and Ward Attendant. One Onge namely- Kwaku of Dugong Creek is deaf and dumb and he has been provided with a hearing aid after an intensive examination by ENT Specialist at Port Blair. At Dugong Creek a helipad has been constructed to airlift the serious patient for treatment at Hut Bay or Port Blair.

At South Bay Settlement three wells are used as source of drinking water, while in the settlement of Dugong Creek, drinking water through pipelines is supplied to the Govt. quarters and the wells used by the Onges are chlorinated in both the settlements timely.

On experimental basis a piggery unit was established in 1983. Boars, sows, bucks, milch she goats, pairs of milch cow with oxen were given to the Onges. In October 1999 a Backyard Poultry Unit (Giri Rani) has been introduced among the Onge. The Department of Animal Husbandry and Veterinary Services has supplied these birds with available guidance of a Veterinary doctor to the Onges. A goatry unit has also been established for Onge welfare. A Police Wireless unit, community hall, Guest house, Footpath from jetty to Onge Settlement and a passenger hall with jetty (1982) have been established at Dugong Creek for the welfare of the Onges.

Regarding the extent of forest areas, out of total 732 sq. km., 500 sq.km. is Tribal Reserve declared in 1956 for the Onges. Thereafter some land from denotified area was converted into Revenue land. No outsider without permission from the concerned authority is allowed to enter the 'Tribal Reserve' area. As far as Tribal pass for the Onge territory is concerned under section 7 of the Andaman & Nicobar Islands (Protection of Aboriginal Tribes) Regulation, 1956, the Deputy Commissioner is empowered to grant such pass. He has issued only 17 passes from 1995 to 1999.

The timber harvesting being carried out in Little Andaman Island is neither arbitrary nor faulty and rather is based upon technical and scientific consideration and assessments. The timber is harvested in these groups of isles by practicing a time tested silvicultural system known as Andaman Canopy Lifting Shelter Wood System. Under this scheme no clear felling is resorted to and only mature and over mature trees are selectively harvested.

The Department of Forest has made all efforts for protection and growth of the rare species like wild pig (*Sus andamanensis*), Giant Robber Crab (*Birgus latro*), Andaman Teal (*Anas gibberifrons albogularis*), Salt water crocodile (*Crocodiles porosus*), the Giant leather back or leathery turtle (*Dermochelys cariacea*), the Green sea turtle (*Chelonia mydas*) and the Dugong.

The Onges still perform the following rituals.

a) Beenjami Gay Kayabee (burial ritual)

b) Ge Angachibe (marriage)

c) Aale Ge Ootoke (birth ceremony)

d) Gay borata Ge Tambo Nuna
Totoreka (pig hunting)

e) Tanaguru (ritual of adulthood)

f) Narelange Totoreka (turtle hunting)

g) Kekonoea, Totereka (Crab hunting)

h) Bogluba (fishing)

i) Weeya (Clay painting).

The Onge and Great Andamanese are provided with the monthly free ration items on a prescribed scale as given below:

Table 7 : The Monthly free Ration items for Onge and Great Andamanese

Sl.No	Name of Items	Quantity (per head)
1.	Rice	9 K.G
2.	Wheat flour	5 K.G
3.	Sugar	500 grams
4.	Pulse	-do-
5.	Dalda	-do-
6.	Edible oil	-do-
7.	Tea leaves	-do-
8.	Onion	-do-
9.	Milk powder	-do-
10.	Coriander powder	50 grams
11.	Tamarind	-do-
12.	Turmeric powder	-do-
13.	Chilly powder	-do-
14.	Salt	500 grams
15.	Bathing soap	2 Nos.
16.	Washing soap	2 Nos.
17.	Candle	1 pkt.
18.	Match box	2 Nos.

Supplementary food to infants upto the age of 3 years.

Baby milk 2 kg. (per month per head)

Cerelac 1 kg (per month per head)

Besides the supply of monthly free ration items annual free cloths also given to them as per the following: -

2 sets of shirt and shorts for male and

2 sets of *lungi* and blouses for female.

The child and maternity care have been undertaken by the responsible authority. The studies pertaining to health and nutritional status of the Onges have been conducted by the scholars and experts on behalf of the Andaman and Nicobar Administration and other agencies.

With reference to the ecological maintenance the plantation of coconut cum-orchard has been raised in Onge Settlement. The coconut plantation at Dugong Creek was damaged badly by the cyclonic storm of December 1976. The damaged plantation has since been renovated and seedlings in large quantity were planted. Margosa and large Casuarina trees were also planted in Onge areas.

For the facility of accommodation of the Primitive Tribes at Port Blair a transit home known as 'Adibasera' has been constructed under the 5th Five Year Plan in 1976 at Port Blair to provide with them shelter when they are at Port Blair.

A Post Office saving scheme has been introduced among the Onges in 1979. Some of the Onges are engaged in clearing and maintenance work of the settlements on daily wage basis. They were also encouraged to raise kitchen gardens in the settlements. One Onge male has been engaged in Medical Sub-Centre, another one in powerhouse on consolidated pay. One Onge Mr. Ramu was working as Jettyman at Dugong Creek employed by the Directorate of Shipping Services, Port Blair but unfortunately he died of an accident (killed by an elephant). Two Onge men Intogage and Mohan Lall were employed as Constables in Department of Police.

Besides all the welfare activities undertaken for the Onge welfare, the Onge still go to fish hunt and collect sea and forest produces regularly.

At present the total population of Great Andamanese in number is 47. It is steadily increased population, which was only 19 before they were resettled on a separate island called 'Strait Island' in 1969. They were provided with all possible facilities for their growth and protection in the settlement by the Andaman & Nicobar Administration. Before their resettlement they were living in dilapidated Japanese bunkers in unhygienic condition at Port Blair and living in other islands too. The monthly free ration items on a prescribed scale are supplied to them as it is provisioned for the Onges. These free ration items supplied are in addition to their indigenous food items from the hunting, fishing and gathering activities. In the indigenous dietary menu of the Great Andamanese Pork, fish, dugong, turtle, turtle eggs, crab, venison, molluscs, roots and tubers etc. are included even today. They have well learnt the preparation of the items prevailed in the neighbouring so called civilized society like dal, rice, chapatti, vegetables, kheer (rice boiled with sugar and milk) sweet dishes etc. To improve the nutritional status of the tribals Goatry and Poultry units have been established in the settlement. In addition to it Girirani variety of poultry has been introduced among the tribals. Agriculture Department is raising kitchen gardens in the settlement. A coconut plantation-cum-orchard has been raised in the Great Andamanese settlement. The coconut trees have been distributed family-wise equally among them. The tribes collect the nuts, consume it and the surplus produce are sold out. A Co-operative Society namely "Great Andamanese Multi Purpose Co-operative Society (GAMPCS)" has been formed in 1977, but the society now has limited functions owing to limited shares.

More than 13 Nos. of cows and calves were introduced among the Great Andamanese but as observed the tribals did not look after the animals. The tribal youths and adults were engaged in clearing and maintenance of the settlement on daily wages. The cash allowances were given to the Great Andamanese. Before being posted to the Shompen Hut Complex at Great Nicobar Island the author has worked among the Great Andamanese in their settlement for nearly a year in 2002-03.

One Primary School has been established on 11.01.1991, which now has been converted into Middle school recently. In the Middle School there are two teachers with 12 students enrolled. There are 2,2,1,5 and 2 students in classes Ist, IInd, IIIrd, VIth &VIIth respectively. The Central Institute of Indian Languages, Mysore has prepared the premiers for the tribal children in Great Andamanese-Hindi-English language in 1994-95.

A solar power plant of 15 kW and a Diesel Power Generator were installed on 20.05.1993 and 25.06.1982 respectively.

A better-equipped dispensary with all time compounder was opened in the settlement in 1969. A Medical Officer visit the settlement from a neighboring island called 'Long Island' to take care of the health of the Great Andamanese. In the very beginning de-addiction was started for 13 opium addicts in a phased manner and now there is no opium addict in the settlement.

Previously two fishing boats (mechanized) were provided with other boating materials and some of the tribal members were given training pertaining to boating. Fishing requisites (fishing nets, hook, fishing lines, etc.) were also supplied to the Great Andamanese.

A Community hall has been constructed in the settlement in 1969 and a Direct Receiving Set (DRS) TV has been placed in the community hall. The police Radio Station was established on 26.09.1986. A cemented footpath has been laid between the jetty and all the houses and service centers in the settlement.

Some of the Great Andamanese were employed as Attendant in Medical Sub-Center, Helper in Powerhouse and Balwadi teacher in Strait Island on consolidated monthly pay. Shri Loka-I (Late) served during the British period in Forest Department. Also he served in Bush Police. Shri Biye (Late) served as Seaman in British boat; he served in Forest Department also. Late Biye, Late Illfe (Surmai's father), Late Kota and Late Maro also served in the Bush police. They died in different years. Late Nao (Sr.) and Shri Jirake (the present chief of the community) had served in Bush Police and Marine department respectively. At present Shri Joe, Shri Sullu, Shri Mayo, Shri Gullat and many other Great Andamanese are employed in Govt. sectors. Smti. Leechu, Smti. Noe and Smti. Kaba are the female Great Andamanese members who employed in different government sectors.

A post office saving scheme has been introduced among the Great Andamanese.

A fully equipped team of field functionaries has been in action after the setting of the settlement to look after the autochthons and implement the welfare schemes.

The cemented wells have been constructed to provide drinking water with the tribes. These wells are chlorinated timely to purify the drinking water. The items like fan, mosquito net, implements, household items and other items of the tribal demand are supplied to the Great Andamanese as and when they require by the AAJVS.

Whenever any ritual is performed by the Great Andamanese, the AAJVS duly extend all possible financial and physical helps to the tribal members. On most of the tribal ceremonies the AAJVS sent its representative(s) to attend the ceremony and record the same.

Now the Great Andamanese cast their votes in the Lok Sabha Election under the Indian Democratic System. The sporting activities have also been introduced among the Great Andamanese.

Handling the Primitive Jarawa tribe is a vexed issue and the Andaman and Nicobar Administration is trying to tackle it with a cautious approach. What the local administration is utmost conscious of is the health and hygiene of the Jarawa community. The all administrative efforts towards the Jarawa are to help them live their own life without disturbing them adversely with taking care of their health, growth and protection. The present population of the Jarawa in number is around 350 (author's enumeration).

The Andaman & Nicobar Administration had been making efforts to establish friendly relationship with the Jarawas and Sentinelese. Periodically contact expeditions were conducted to befriend the said two tribal communities by the official team. The first successful contact with the Jarawas was established in February 1974. Since our present understanding of the Jarawa community is not sufficient enough to warrant any long-term policy measure, at this juncture a seminar on *'Future Policy Towards the Primitive Tribes'* was organized by AAJVS in December 1995 at Port Blair. In pursuance of the recommendations of the seminar a six month Pilot Project to have a deeper insight into the Jarawa life was launched from September 1996. The contacts with the Sentinelese were also intensified. A project to study the Jarawa language has been assigned to CIIL in which encouraging initial success has been made.

Recently one Jarawa boy namely 'Enmay' incidentally got his leg fractured at Kadamtala and he was brought to GB Pant Hospital, Port Blair for treatment. During the period of his treatment at Port Blair the official side served the best service with extra care to Enmay in respect of food and behaviour. After his treatment he was sent back to his habitat with plenty of gift items. After this happening, the Jarawa started coming out of their forest in groups understanding the good service rendered towards Enmay. This phenomenon has minimized the expedition to befriend the Jarawas.

But the coming out of the forest by the Jarawas and causing disturbance to the non-autochthons has served a new challenge to the official side particularly the AAJVS to tackle it with great care. In the recent years the Jarawa started coming frequently on the 'Andaman Trunk Road' and to some adjacent non-tribal settlements of Middle and South Andaman. Their curiosity towards the outsiders after the Enmay Case perhaps brought them out of their natural dwelling and in contacts with the outsiders usually they beg for food and other items mainly for the reason that they know that these wanted items the outsiders can give to them as they gave on previous occasions to Enmay and other Jarawas.

To prevent the Jarawa mishap towards the outsiders the representatives of AAJVS and Jarawa Protection Police (JPP) are making their best efforts to control the Jarawa movement and to stop Jarawa intrusion into the adjacent settlements. The Jarawa enter into the adjacent settlements to take away their required items like iron, vessel, banana, implements etc. The field functionaries of AAJVS provide with the Jarawa these said items as and when required to stop this. The Jarawas are shifted from the revenue area of their appearance to their actual habitat in Jarawa Reserve to avoid any unwanted situation and sometimes they are shifted from their own one camp to another at their will avoiding the Jarawa mixing with outsiders.

It has also been observed that the Jarawa quite often appear on ATR either to contact the non-Jarawas or to board the tops of plying buses (Totkli in Jarawa language). To prevent the Jarawa from boarding the buses and other vehicles and to bring more frequency in patrolling recently two mini trucks have been purchased by the AAJVS and deployed on Andaman Trunk Road on 19.10.2000 to shift the Jarawas avoiding the outside contact from one place to another as and when required. To have close watch on the Jarawas and their movements and to control the complex / unwanted situation created by the Jarawa and to implement the Jarawa welfare schemes at ground level, the AAJVS has appointed a Tribal Welfare Officer at Kadamtala of Middle Andaman and a Plantation-in-charge with an assisting staff at Baratang who are timely assisted by the JPPs and the officials of other departments like APWD, Department of health Services, Department of Forest etc.

During the first week of October 2000 a Jarawa group of 15-20 members from Tirur area (South Andaman) reached Punnanallah area on ATR side and constructed a new hut there. Looking to this new situation the AAJVS conducted a series of patrolling for ten continuous days in the Jarawa areas particularly on ATR. Apart from it they were given banana and coconut in adequate quantity as preventive measure against their coming into contact with the outsiders for want of food.

Jarawas are still unpredictable. When and through which way they are to move, the outsiders cannot determine. Despite the close watch on their movement reportedly on many occasions the Jarawas have entered the nearby settlements and looted their belongings like banana, iron, vessel, tools and implements. But in most of the Jarawa raids into the non-tribal settlements mainly the Jarawa plundered the bananas from the gardens. The supply of gift items of the Jarawa like is the main preventive measure against the Jarawa intrusion into the adjacent settlements and against their coming into contact with the outsiders for want of above said items. Many villagers have filed their request for grant of relief amount against the damage of their property caused by the Jarawas. After necessary verification several such villagers have been granted the relief amount (70% of the sustained total cost of damage caused by Jarawa) by the AAJVS. A Public Awareness Camp has been organized by the author on behalf of the AAJVS at Kadamtala on 06th October, 2000 to betterment the autochthon and non-autochthon relationship looking to their bitter thinking and rough knowledge about the Jarawas.

In order to augment the food resources in the Jarawa territory, schemes of dispersed plantation, sea ranching, project pig and installation of fish aggregation device have been implemented.

Under the dispersed plantation seedlings to provide various kinds of fruit were planted in Jarawa Reserve. With the help of the Department of Agriculture 50 banana, 100 coconuts, 25 guava and 25 jackfruit seedlings were raised at Jarawa area during June 1999. In the same year on 15.09.1999, 25 Nos. seedlings of fruit bearing trees were raised. Later on many occasions seedlings to enrich the Jarawa reserve with food resources were planted. In the Jarawa concentrated area like Lakra Lungta and Spike Island the coconut seedlings were raised in favour of the tribes. As per another record 325 Nos. of seedlings of fruit bearing trees were planted between March'99 and August'99 at Jarawa area. Under the program of Sea ranching on 03.02.99 molluscs were released into the shallow water of Lakra Lungta and gillnets were distributed to the Jarawas. On 02.03.1999, 220 Nos. of molluscs were broadcasted in the creeks and fishing nets tied at R. K. Nallah and B.D Nallah and demonstrated the art of fishcatch to the Jarawa tribes. Subsequently on 14.05.1999, 250 Nos. of molluscs have been released at P. K. Nallah. Apart from it fish aggregation artificial traps have been installed at Lakra Lungta area for the benefit of the Jarawa. Fishing materials like hooks, nets etc. have also been supplied to them.

As far as the medical coverage is concerned, the Jarawas have shown considerable interest in the modern modes of treatment. Since September 1995 there have been more than one thousand cases of Jarawa treatment recorded till this date. During this period the Jarawa patients were treated in GB Pant Hospital,

Port Blair, Primary Health Centre Tushnabad, Primary Health Centre, Kadamtala and at different Jarawa habitats like Lakra Lungta, Foul Bay, Dhaninallah and Jhaukona, etc.

To serve comfortable and eco-friendly environment and special care and facilities to the admitted Jarawa patients, 2 exclusive Jarawa wards of ten beds have been established at Primary Health Centre Kadamtala and Primary Health Centre Tushnabad.

Recently a handbook on Jarawa language has been prepared by the Central Institute of Indian Languages, Mysore, the copies of which have been distributed among the field functionaries to bring more proficiency in their work avoiding the language barrier.

To assess the Jarawa situation and other related issues through a contemporary discussion and reach an appropriate decision a Task Force Committee chaired by the Lieutenant Governor as been constituted with the following members.

1. Principal, Chief Conservator of Forests, Port Blair.
2. Secretary (Tribal Welfare), A & N Administration, Port Blair.
3. Director of Health Services, A & N Administration, Port Blair.
4. Director (Tribal Welfare), A & N Administration, Port Blair.
5. Deputy Commissioner (Andamans).
6. Superintendent of Police (Andamans)
7. Head of Office, Anthropological Survey of India, Port Blair.
8. Executive Secretary, AAJVS, Port Blair - Convenor.

The Hon'ble Lieutenant Governor, A & N Islands has constituted a 'Research and Development Cell' to advice the administration to handle the complex situation (if any created) and to advice on the concerned various issues from time to time to reach a firmed policy or decision for Jarawa Welfare. This cell comprises of the following members under the chairpersonship of the Hon'ble Lieutenant Governor, A & N Islands:

1. Head of Office, Anthropological Survey of India, Port Blair.
2. Director, Central Institute of Indian Languages, Mysore.
3. Principal Chief Conservator of Forest, Port Blair.
4. Director of Health Services, A & N Administration, Port Blair.
5. Director, Regional Medical Research Centre (ICMR), Port Blair.
6. Director of Tribal Welfare, A & N Administration, Port Blair.
7. Executive Secretary, AAJVS – Convenor.

Under the present policy the Andaman and Nicobar Administration does not allow itself to be rushed into any hasty ill-conceived programme which would have an undesirable effect on the self-reliance and culture of the Jarawa, the foragers. The fact is well understood that they are not at all uninvited guests, they have equal rights like any other citizen of India for protection of life and personal liberty and the local administration has followed certain policy sincerely raising the level of nutrition and the standard of living and to improve the health without disturbing the tribes adversely.

The general public opined before me during my stay at a village near to Jarawa Reserve that food starvation mainly leads the Jarawas to come out of the forest which is absolutely incorrect. The Jarawa intrusion into the neighbouring villages is not due to the food starvation but many facts can be well attributed to it. A tribal has a simple and broad thinking, that is why after their xenophobia has gone away instead of going deep into the forest or sea in search of food, they think going to adjacent villages at night and collecting banana, iron, implements etc. is much easier job. Their increased curiosity and fun are also added to the reason. The history also says that the Jarawa's coming into the neighbouring settlements is not new. After the 'Enmay Case', a highly increased curiosity towards the outsiders among the Jarawas brought them out of the forest with no fear. It is obvious from the recent events when 15-20 curious Jarawas from Tirur of South Andaman appeared on ATR, constructed hut on ATR side, stayed for few weeks and then returned back to their actual habitats. This clearly reflects the fact that they did nct come on ATR owing to food starvation in their reserve.

It has been observed that few of the Jarawa community have well learnt the use of soap, hair oil and towels, while many of them started wearing clothes and bathing properly. The hospital and PHCs have become a ground for our observation of such practices by the Jarawas. Remarkably they are not forced to practice such things.

From moral point of view also the administration has shown keen interest and special care towards the Jarawa tribe. Recently one Jarawa boy aged 5-6 years namely '*Tangato*' was found neglected and injured on ATR side. Immediately he was brought under medical treatment. The further investigation revealed that this Jarawa boy was an orphan and living in great negligence among the Jarawas. The official team found after an intensive inquiry that there was a maternal uncle of the boy namely Shri *Noru.* He was further persuaded to accept the boy and take care of him. Now the boy lives with his maternal uncle.

In July 2000 through a circular from Director (Tribal Welfare), addressing officially the Jarawa tribe as 'hostile' has been completely banned.

Sentinelese are still living an isolated life inhabiting the North Sentinel Island. Till recently periodical contact expeditions have been conducted to befriend the tribe. During the expedition hours the gift items like banana, coconut, iron etc. were given to them. They are perhaps the most untouched Negrito foragers in the World today.

5

Development of Primitive Tribes: The Conceptual Frame

The problem of defining 'development' becomes more acute when one tries to apply the concept in a tribal context. Different people have given different interpretations, while some have considered a holistic approach as the basis of development, others have felt that this need not necessarily be so. There has been three main streams of thinking regarding the approach to tribal development – isolation, assimilation and gradual integration.

In the new strategy of development, the two concepts viz. a very backward stage of economic development and lower level in the economic structure have been clearly distinguished. Those groups in the later category are termed as the more backward tribal communities.

Agricultural economy as been taken to be the watershed for identification of Primitive Tribal communities. The pre-agricultural economic groups generally have been included in the Primitive communities. The highest form of technology in the case of these groups can be said to be practiced by shifting cultivators. In defining Primitive Tribal Groups, some more distinguishing features have to be identified. It appears that literacy is an important criterion, which may reasonably indicate the general level of social development of a community. Therefore besides the stage of economy, level of literacy has been taken as a characteristic to identify the Primitive Tribal communities.

As far as the PTGs of Andaman and Nicobar Islands are concerned, the modern education is far away from them. The stage of human life and technology are the chief contirbutors towards their identification and group specification. They are still living a primitive stage of life on earth having the primitive technology of nearly stone age.

At present there are 77 identified Primitive Tribal Groups in different parts of India including the Andaman and Nicobar Islands. The criteria in identifying the groups by the government are:

1. Pre agricultural level of technology.
2. Low level of literacy.
3. Stagnant or diminishing population.

Primitive Tribal Groups are considered vulnerable population due to their small size, isolation, low level of literacy and their nature of subsistence, which is dependent purely on the environment in which they live and require special attention for their protection and growth. Except for a few the rest of these groups can be divided into two categories viz. the groups solely depending on hunting and gathering and the groups depending on hunting, gathering and shifting cultivation.

The total population of Primitive Tribal Groups in India is more than 15 lakh and varies from 47 Great Andamanese to more than 2 lakh strong Seharias of Madhya Pradesh. The Primitive Tribal Groups of Andaman and Nicobar Islands are miniscule in size and are fighting for their survival. These primitive tribes constitute a meagre portion of the total population of the Andaman and Nicobar Islands. But the small Primitive Tribal Groups like Birhor, Kadar, Cholanicken, Raji etc. are also being marginalized. The process of marginalisation of small and Primitive Tribal Groups is going on uninhibited despite constitutional safe-guards, extra and special developmental programmes launched both by the central and state governments.

Planning for total integrated development of primitive tribal communities in India primarily aims at serving in such a manner that there is all round development and progress and in the process inbuilt mechanism gets developed, which not only sustains the achievement but with the passage of time gives the chance of evaluation being in flexibility. Tribal in general has a highly developed social instinct of togetherness. Keeping in view of this a suitable plan is framed.

Tribal milleu is such that life and living are group oriented and unless focus of delivery of services shifts from individual to group, approach will be tardy and pace of progress can not be accelerated. This is very much a fact of life at the Primitive Tribal Group level.

In short Tribal development can not be administered from above; it has to be organized from below. Their sentiments should not be neglected. Development as contrasted with more growth, is a long drawn out process and it has to be viewed on a long term perspective from various vantagepoints – legal, social, cultural, economic etc.

Dr. S. Radhakrishnan, former President of India, who at the time of inaugurating the sixth Tribal Conference at Gotacamund on 21st May 1960 said, *inter alia*:

> "Don't create disturbance in the mental attitudes of people, do not try to unsettle their ways of life, do not make them displaced in their own country. Don't make them orphans, don't make them uprooted but try to teach every one his own particular way of life. We know if we take off people from their tradition, we brutalize them. We make loose their sense of joy. This doesn't, however, mean that we love the status quo, that we do not allow these people to grow. The point is that the growth must be within and should not be imposed from without".

Most of the miniscule and small primitive tribal groups are hunter-gatherers and live in *'Bands'*. Band is an adaptation to the ecological and environmental conditions of their respective habitats.

These groups are tightly knit and practice generalized reciprocity. The worldview is limited to their foraging area and its environment. Everything falling beyond their worldview is strange and they even perceive it as dangerous. Egalitarianism, situational leadership, no structural political organization except respecting the aged, etc. also characterize these groups. These types of groups are not amenable to sudden change. Their habitat and its environment becomes absolute property of the community and no restrictions are placed on any member to eke out his / her subsistence. Their traditional right and freedom of exploitation of resources does not mean over exploitation, they take from the environment strictly according to their immediate needs. This type of utilization may be called *'Sustainable subsistence'* or *'Eco-friendly subsistence'* or *'Subsistence economy'*. Due to centuries of occupation these groups develop a primordial sense of attachment to their habitats. Cultural intimacy with their habitats is found among all the indigenous and tribal populations apparently. Among them their habitat and environment are considered as sacred and linked closely with moral and spiritual perspectives. All the developmental strategies should have these tribal values a firm place in consideration.

The tribal development strategy had been subjected to close scrutiny from plan to plan and had undergone finer tuning and orientation. It was during the concept of Tribal Sub-Plan (Tribal Sub-Plan) implemented. The essential features of Tribal Sub-Plan are:

- Recognize that there is no uniform solution to the variety of problems facing the tribal regions and tribal communities; therefore, accept the uniqueness and formulate policies, programmes and schemes to suit each individual situation.
- Evolve appropriate frame for development with emphasis on tribal people at the national and state level through the Sub-Plan exercise, ensuring adequate quantification from state and central plan funds, with budgetary mechanisms to ensure accountability, non-divertability and utilization.

- Accord highest priority to protective measures for elimination of exploitation of tribal people.
- Restructure the administrative and institutional setup to suit the local needs and aspirations.
- Supplement state efforts substantially by the Union government.[29]

The Tribal Sub-Plan (TSP) is a part and parcel of the national plan. It envisages all round development of the tribal areas in an interpreted measure. The TSP represents totality of efforts and comprises of four elements, viz. the flow of investments from the State Plan, the Central Ministries / Departments, Special Central Assistance controlled by the Ministry of Human Affairs and institutional finance. The TSP strategy was started in 1975-76 in a most form with an investment of about 13 crores, and it was operational in Andaman & Nicobar Islands since 1978 onwards and since then a considerable number of schemes have been implemented under it.

A strategy for economic development of the Andaman & Nicobar Islands has to withstand two extreme and opposing points of view. The ecological and environmental school would by and large like these islands to remain as they are and oppose any development that would interfere with the tropical raintrees – said to be in their last refuge – and the fragile soil formation of these islands or the tribal character of a few of them. At the other extreme is a school of thought which would like these islands to be developed on the pattern of Hongkong or Singapore, that is to say a macropolis type of economic development with a duty free export production zone, and offshore banking center and also a market for consumer goods. A correct strategy will seek to initiate changes whose nature and tempo will have to be determined by ecological and environmental constraints. Anything, which disturbs adversely the vegetation, the topography, soil formation and the savagers, must be avoided. All development efforts must be modest, gradual and totally in tune with the environment.

Anthropologists (like some environmentalists) have been quite often blamed for advocating protectionist human 300 concepts for the tribals. There is no doubt that the five small primitive tribes of Andaman & Nicobar Islands are among the beleaguered human communities. They need to be protected and looked after by responsible official agencies under proper scientific supervision and guidance so that they not only survive but live as self-respecting communities. Also they must not be hustled into getting hopelessly embroiled in the '*mainstream conceptual vulgarity*'.

In 1986 Govt. of India had appointed a high power committee of experts to recommend special measures for these small tribes of Andaman & Nicobar Islands. The committee chaired by Dr. S.C Sinha met several times, visited these tribes and recommended to appoint a team of well chosen specialists under a leader who would actually involve themselves in research, planning and monitoring all new measures involving the people themselves at all stages (and treating their values, views and opinions with respect) so that highly sensitive tribal touchable programmes could be evolved and implemented successfully.

In all fairness it has to be said that no general guideline can be suggested for all the groups for obvious reasons. Each group will demand separate treatment. Active participation of representatives of the tribal group in formulation of plans at all stages at possible level is a sine quo non for its success and implementation. Every endeavour should be made to locate available persons amongst the group and take them into confidence.

In various parts of the world tribal people have reacted, to the best to their ability in one of the following ways, when confronted with modern civilization and allied aspects; they have "(1) totally ignored it; (2) deliberately avoided it; or (3) responded with defiant arrogance. Any of these responses clearly could be interpreted as an open rejection of further involvement with progress" (Bodley, 1982: 16).

Australian Aborigines showed no interest at all in the ship and other possessions of Captain Cook and his men. Elkin confirms this attitude of the Aborigines – there was a total lack of interest in white people's customs, belief and possessions and the Aborigines believed that the whites were temporary visitors and would soon leave them (Aborigines) to lead their own lives undisturbed (1951).

In the Andaman Islands only the Sentinelese have been able to avoid the first hand "contact". The avoiding responses of the Primitive Tribes are to be intensively studied from all corners to reach a new answer to the failure of scheme (if any) and suggest alternatives. Such study may also help to understand the root factors of the problems.

A primitive tribal community represents an earlier stage of our socio-economic life. In the earlier stage of human society, the pace of change was very slow. The human society was in that stage even in Neolithic period. The Neolithic period is pertaining to the last period of the Stone Age (succeeding the Paleolithic and Mesolithic) from about 6000 to 3000 BC in Europe and western Asia, when Neoliths came into use as well as implements of polished bone and horn, animals came to be domesticated, crops cultivated, weaving undertaken and the wheel used. The long Barrows and Megaliths of Britain are associated with this cultural period. The Andaman tribes are still at the socio-economic and cultural stage of Pre-Neolithic period, because using of wheel, crop cultivation and domestication of animal have been unknown to these foragers. Therefore bringing sudden change among these small primitive groups, who have been largely stabled for the past thousands of years, may cause tribal damage severely.

The overall assessment of the activities undertaken for the welfare of the primitive tribes of these isles reveal the fact that no development activity will succeed unless exploitation by outside force in various forms is prevented.

REFERENCES

1. Venkatesan, D: The Andaman-Hunter and Collectors in Shashi, S.S (Ed.), *Island Tribes of Andaman and Nicobar*, Anmol Publications (Pvt.) Ltd, New Delhi, 1995, pp. 4-5.

2. Iqbal Singh, N., *The Andaman Story*, Vikas Publishing House Pvt. Ltd, New Delhi, 1978, p.58
3. *Ibid.*, P. 59
4. Lal, Premanand, *Andaman Islands- A regional geography*, Anthropological Survey of India, Calcutta, 1976, pp. 66-67.
5. Iqbal Singh, N., *op. cit.*, p.143
6. Basu, B.K., *The Onge*, Seagullbooks, Calcutta,1990.
7. Iqbal Singh, N., *op. cit.*, pp.151.
8. Basu, B.K., *op. cit.*, p.11.
9. Iqbal Singh, N., *op. cit.*, pp 158-59.
10. General Report, Census of India, 1931.
11. Iqbal Singh, N, *op.cit.*, p.290.
12. Swamy, P, *Frontline*, Oct. 18, 1996, p.117.
13. Iqbal Singh, N., *op. cit.*, p.60.
14. *Ibid.*, p.60.
15. Singh, K.S., *People of India* Vol.XII (Ed), Anthropological Survey of India, Madras, 1994, p.75.
16. Pandit, T.N., The Sentinelese, Seagull Books, Calcutta, 1990, p.17.
17. Singh, N.I, *op. cit.*, pp.63-64.
18. Sudarsen, V., *Andaman and Nicobar Islands – Challenges of Development* (Ed) Konark Publishers Pvt. Ltd, Delhi, 1994, pp.82-83.
19. Basu, B.K., *op. cit.*, p.24.
20. *Ibid.*, p. 41.
21. *Ibid.*, p.57
22. Iqbal Singh, N., *op. cit.*, pp.153-154.
23. Mann, R.S., *The Bay Islander*, Institute of Social Research and Applied Anthropology, Calcutta, 1991, pp. 23-24.
24. Iqbal Singh, N., *op. cit.*, p 162.
25. Sarkar, J., *The Jarawa*, Seagull Books, Calcutta, 1990, p.38.
26. Iqbal Singh, N., *op. cit.*, p.154.
27. Rizvi, S.N.H., *The Shompen*, Seagullbooks, Calcutta, 1990, p.9.
28. *Ibid.*, p.12.
29. Menon, P.S.K., *Tribal Development – Policies, Plans and Programs in Yojana* (Vol. 44 No.4), New Delhi, 2000, p.37.

INDEX

A

AAJVS, 88, 99, 112, 119, 120, 122
Aborigines, 8, 23, 132
Aetas, 8
African slaves, 8
Agricultural economy, 126
Aka-bea tribes, 14
Andaman and Nicobar Islands Integrated Development Corporation, 26
Animals, 3
Arakan Yoma Range of Myanmar 4
Archipelago, 1
Assam valley, 18
Attitude of the aborigines, 132
Australian aborigines, 131

B

Bands, 128
Bantu language, 11
Barrows and Magaliths of Britain, 132
Battle of Aberdeen, 14, 15
Bille Admiral Steen, 95
Biosphere Reserve, 4
Birds 3
Birhor, 127
Blair (Capt.), 16
British colonists, 9, 12
Brown, Radcliff, 8, 66
Burma, 18

C

Cadell (Col.), 19, 23
Capital, 2
Car Nicobar, 1
Cellular Jail, 17
Cholanicken, 127
Cipriani, Lideo, 8, 9
Climate, 5
Climbers, 2
Coastal ecosystem, 3
Colebrook, Robert Hyde, 16, 20, 66
Colonization, 13
Comprising of 572 Islands, 1
Concept of Tribal Sub-Plan, 129
Convict districts, 26
Convicts, 17, 25
Cretaceous period, 7

D

Danes, 13
Davies, Nelson, 17
Desai, Morarji, 14

E

East India Company, 13
Egalitarianism, 129
Elwin, 109
Endangered species, 3
Enmay, 86
Era is Cenozoic, 7
Evergreen trees, 2

Exclusive Economic Zone, 2

F

Fairness, 130

Features of Tribal Sub-Plan, 129

Fields, C.G., 80

Firns, 3

First battle by 200 Anamanese (1859), 15

– penal settlement (1789-96), 13, 16

Free districts, 25

G

Genetic researchers, 12

– studies, 11

Genomic studies, 10

Geographical distribution, 5

Ghosh, A.K., 26

Great Andamanese, 6, 22, 68, 115, 117, 119
 Aberdeen School, 32
 adolescence ceremony, 41
 bands, 34
 believe in mythical beings, 45
 bronchial pulmonary infections, 31
 burial system, 41
 children, 48
 Christian missionaries, 46
 communal hut, 34
 consanguineous marriage, 40
 covering of grave, 43
 death rituals, 42
 decorate their bodies, 38
 Diseases, 31
 division of labour, 43
 enigmaic of human races, 29
 epidemic in 1868, 31
 evil spirit *Jirmu*, 46
 fishing, 43
 food, 35-36
  habits, 46
 forest department, 33
 free ration, 36, 37
 funeral system, 41
 gathering, 43
 graveyard, 42
 hair, 28
 hostile Andamanese, 30
 hostility, 29
 hunting, 43
 kitchen garden, 36
 language *Koro*, 34, 42
 legends and mythical powers, 45
 marriage ceremony, 38-40
 – permitted for widows, widowers, and divorces, 41
 Negrito tribes, 28
 ornaments, 43
 out station home, 31
 penal colonies, 32
 population, 32
 Puluga (God), 45
 religion, 44, 45
 skin colour, 28
 South African Khoisan, 29
 spirit *Biliku*, 46
 – *Tharaye*, 45
 stay naked, 37
 strait island, 33, 34
 – island, 42
 sun burial, 41
 syphilitic sores, 31, 32
 territorial division, 33
 Tomo, 45
 tradition learning, 34
 Viper home, 31
 way of life, 29
 women, 28, 37
 workshop, 44

H

Hunt any pig in the forest, 71

Hunter-gatherers, 128

I

Indian Munity of 1857, 13

IRDP, 25

J

Japanese, 14
Jarawas, 6, 9, 17, 21, 22, 68, 90, 119, 121, 123, 125
AAJVS, 99
aanotahe, 72
aao, 74
abduction, 102
Abo, 104
administration, 99
adolescent ceremony the boy, 75
advent of dog, 100
Aegania, 97
ahav, 98
always distrusted the Great Andamanese, 80
apiculture, 100
APWD workers, 84
armlet is called '*Oetahe*', 72
bee hive, 72
befriended by the outsiders, 74
believe in the existence of malevolent and benevolent spirits, 103
Bimuchadda, 88
both sexes go complete naked, 72
Buaeia, 93
canoes, 67
Chadda de Thuma, 70
commodities of their requirement, 100
community hut, 70, 74
consume cooked food, 72
Danish missionary, 95
dead is buried, 102
– of a person, 78
– – small child, 78
dispose of a dead inside the forest, 78
divisions and bands, 73, 99
– of labour, 73
do not kill the piglings, 100
economic activities, 73
– system, 99
Eeng (water), 75
eldest male member, 103
encounter with the Jarawas, 69
engrave geometric designs on their bow, 76
Enmay Case, 85
exchange, 102
ferocious tribes, 65
fights between Jarawas and non-Jarawas, 21
fire-generatore, 101
first preganancy, 76
fishing, 73, 100
flesh of frog, 97
folk songs, 73
gathering, 100
good swimmer, 73
habitat/location, 90
hanoom, 101
harvest the honey, 100
has no special ritual related to pregnancy, 102
Hatho, 75
health practices, 76
hostility, 68
housing, 95
hunting, 73, 100
– of pig, 100
illegal contact, 99
incidents of marriage between Shompen and non-Shompen, 102
indigenous diet, 96
Indirect Barter, 100
iron, 75
Kachaam, 97
Kanau, 97
kangapo, 72
keep pig fat, 70
Keyet, 93
kinds of economy, 99
kinship, 79

kitchen, 98
know the art of the bow and arrow, 101
known and Sentinelese, 66
Koken, 104
Kontoka, 65
language, 68, 97
Levchadda, 88
local, 99
Luevirate, 102
Mahu, 71
main settlement of outsiders, 82
making outrigger canoe, 101
mala, 98
man, 94
marriage, 98, 102
means strangers, 65
men, 98
mishap towards the outsider, 120
Mongoloid primitive tribes, 93
monogamy, 102
moon (*taape*), 76
murders of the convicts, 80
name themselves as *Aang*, 65
negotiation, 102
Negroid tribes, 65
no racial difference between a Shompen and other Nicobarese, 94
not bury their dead, 78
of recent years and now, 85
Onog, 75
Opemame ceremony of girl, 75
original inhabitants, 94
orphan children, 103
patho, 74
polygyny, 102
population, 69
primitive stage of life on earth, 71
produce fire by a primitive method, 101
Protection Police (JPP), 120
punitive expedition, 80
resin torch, 77
reserve, 111
restrictions on the pregnant woman, 102
rituals pertaining to the birth, marriage and death, 77
Rosen, Pastor, 95
Rudraksha, 98, 100
settlement pattern, 95
Shompen hand, 93
short stature with yellow and yellow-brown skin and wavy hair, 94
shot down several forest and APWD, 84
skulls of wild boars can be seen hanged in a Jarawa Hut, 71
sky (*pangne*), 76
social organization based on tradition, 103
sororate, 102
stars (*chilope*), 76
status of women, 99
sun (ehey), 76
Thom, 75
Thorkalong Chadda, 70
Thosulatetoha, 75
thule, 70
tidings of death, 78
Towa, 74
towards friendship, 79
trade relations with the Nicobarese, 103
traditional medicines, 76
Tuichadda, 88
Tullichadda, 88
Tutime chadda, 70
unmixed origin, 94
unpredictable, 82
use Brochette of iron rod/bamboo to boil fish, 101
– spear, 101
– the juice of pinanga leaves, 100
wayetahe, 72
women, 98
wood cane, 75

K

Kadar, 127
Kazhakh, 10
Kirghiz, 10
Kitchen-midden, 9

L

Lembas, 11
Little Anadaman, 19, 17
Live within the reserve forest area, 69
Lord Cornwallis, 20

M

Mammals 3
Man, Edwaed Horace, 13, 44, 47
Mangrove 3
Melanesians, 9
Mesolithic, 11, 132
Millis, Campbell, 19
Miniscule and small primitive tribal groups, 128
Mitochondrial DNA, 11, 12
Molecula study, 12
Mongoloid racial stock
Moravian missionaries, 13
Morgan, D.L., 69, 80
Mutineers of 1857, 14

N

Naidu, Som, 112
Nallah, R.K., 73
National parks, 4
Negritos, 8, 9
Nehru, Jawaharlal, 110
Neolithic period, 11, 132
Nicobarese, 10

O

Onges, 6, 10, 20, 114, 115
  adolescence rituals, 59
  are nomadic, 49
  bands, 55
  bows and arrows, 56
  call themselves *Eniregale*, 51
  canoes, 56, 64
  communal hut (*beryra*), 51, 55
  concept of religion, 64
  conversion, 19
  cooking food, 51
  – pots, 55
  death rituals, 63-64
  divorce dose not exist, 62
  eat natural food, 52
  edible items, 53
  females, 54
  fish, 52
  fishing, 57
  flesh, which they enjoy, 54
  free ration, 52
  hunter gatherers, 52
  indigenous diet items, 52
  – Onge menu, 52
  leaves of Pandanus provides roofing, 52
  liquor, 54
  Little Andaman, 49
  males, 54, 55
  marriage rituals, 62-63
  monogamous, 62
  mother-naked, 54
  nakinyage, 54
  not tattoo themselves, 54
  only one of their kind in the world, 51
  painting called *alame*, 54
  population, 51
  pregnancy rituals, 58-59
  puberty rituals, 60-62
  pure Negrito tribes, 112
  Pygmies, 51
  resettlement, 64

ritual getenkare, 58
settlement, 114
spirit *onkobowkwe*, 58
spiritual world, 54, 58
syphilis, 19
tanagiru ritual, 59, 60
tools, 57
utensils, 57
women, 55

Origin, 10

Orphanage, 17

P

Palaeolithic colonizers, 12

Palaeolithic, 11, 132

Pandit, T.N., 81

Papuan, 9

Parts of range from Myanmar to Sumatra, 2

Planning for total integrated development, 128

Plants 3

Population, 4, 24, 28

Portman, M.V., 9, 19, 21, 23, 49, 104

Primitive Tribal Groups, 126, 127

Primitive tribes, 5, 6, 8, 10, 27

Ptolemy, 8

R

Radhakrishnan, S., 128

Raji, 127

Reptiles, 3

Reserve forest, 2

S

Sadloo, 15

Schools, 17

Second penal settlement, 14

Seharias of Madhya Pradesh, 127

Semangs, 8

Sensitive tribal touchable programme, 130

Sentinelese, 6, 17, 22, 104
administrative officials, 104
expedition, 106
– under Portman, M.V., 104
first official census, 105
international ships, 105
life of the Sentinelese, 105
naval officers, 104
negrito Sentinelese, 104
politicians, 104
Primrose, M.V., 105
Rusley, M.V., 105
second recorded landing, 104
Shooting with bowarrow, 104
undisputed lords of their island, 106
unrecorded occasional poaching, 105

Shompens 6, 23

Sixth Tribal Conference, 129

Standford University, 12

Stone Age, 132

Strategy for economic development, 130

T

Tanjore inscription, 13

Tasminians, 9

Tehsil-wise population, 5

Temple, R., 94

Temple, Sir Richard, 14, 44

Timber, 2

Tiwari, Doodhnath, 15, 16

Total population 127

Trekkers, 21

Tribal bands, 16

– development strategy, 128, 129

Tribal group, 5
– milleu, 128
– Sub-Plan (TSP), 130
Uighur, 10
Union Jack, 14

V

Victoria Cross, 19
Volcanic islands, 4
Vulnerable population, 127

W

Wahabi convicts, 14
Walker, J.P., 16, 17
Welfare Activities, 109, 111, 116
  aboriginals to the mainland, 110
  Andaman Adim Janjati Vikas Samiti (AAJVS), 112, 119, 120, 122
  A & N Administration, 119
  A & N Islands (Protection of Aboriginal Tribes) Regulation, 1956, 111
  Andaman Canopy, 114
  Awareness Camp, 122
  British and Japanese policy of isolation, 109
  buses, 121
  Bush Police, 118
  cemented wells,119
  Community hall, 118
  Co-operative Society namely, 114, 117
  department of Forest, 114
  diesel Generator, 114
  Direct Receiving Set (DRS) TV, 118
  Director (Tribal Welfare), 125
  establishment of Sort of National Park of the Tribals, 109
  expanding agriculture in the islands, 109
  field functionaries, 118
  forest areas, 114
  – department, 110
  fundamental principles, 110
  GAMPCS, 117
  Gramin Telephone, 112
  handbook on Jarawa language, 123
  health Centre Kadamtala, 123
  – of the Great Andamanese, 118
  Medical officer-in-charge, 115
  Minor Forest Produces (MFPs), 112
  monthly free ration items for Onge and Great Andamanese, 115
  Nallah, B.D., 122
  Nehruvian policy, 111
  period of occupation, 109
  piggery unit, 114
  plight of the tribal communities, 110
  post office, 116, 118
  Primary Health Centre, 123
  Primitive Jarawa, 119
  Rudraksh, 112
  shllow water of Lakra Lungta, 122
  Shompen aspects, 112
  Shompen Hut Complex (SHC), 112, 117
  Som Naidu, 112
  Special Central Assistance (SCA), 112
  species like wild pig, 114
  Task Force Committee, 123
  timber harvesting, 114
  tribal *panchsheel*, 110
  – Reserve, 111, 114
  water, 115
  welfare of the Jarawas, 111
Wildlife, 2, 3
– sanctuaries 4
Wilson, Allan C., 11
World tribal, 131
World War, 1945, 13

Y

Y-chromosomes, 11
Yemen, 11

PLATES

Plate 1. The Great Andamanese being integrated to civilized society.

Plate 2. The Great Andamanese performing death ritual.

Plate 3. A Shompen member.

Plate 4. A Shompen youth.

Plate 5. A Jarawa girl.

Plate 6. A Jarawa youth with his bow and arrow.

Plate 7. A Jarawa girl eating gifted puffed rice.

Plate 8. The Onge children of Dugong Creek.